S0-AIU-107

Orville and Wilbur Wright

PIONEERS OF THE AGE OF FLIGHT

By Diane Dakers

Crabtree Publishing Company

www.crabtreebooks.com

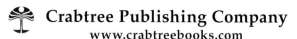

Crabtree Publishing Company
www.crabtreebooks.com

Author: Diane Dakers

Series research and development:
Reagan Miller

Project coordinator: Mark Sachner

Editors: Mark Sachner, Lynn Peppas

Indexer: Gini Holland

Editorial director: Kathy Middleton

Photo research: Crystal Sikkens and
Mark Sachner

Designer: Westgraphix/Tammy West

Proofreader: Kelly Spence

**Production coordinator and
prepress technician:** Ken Wright

Print coordinator: Kathy Berti

Written and produced by Water Buffalo Books

Photographs and reproductions:
Jeff Dakers: pp. 36–37. **Library of Congress:** cover
(foreground), 8 (top), 9 (top), 11, 16, 18, 20 (left and center),
24, 25, 27, 29 (lower right), 33 (lower left, lower middle),
39, 40, 41, 42 (bottom), 43, 44, 45, 46, 46–47, 50, 51, 53
(bottom), 57, 59, 62 (top and bottom), 63 (bottom), 64, 66,
68 (top), 71, 72 (bottom), 73, 75 (both lower), 77, 78 (top),
79 (bottom), 83, 84 (upper), 85 (bottom), 87, 89 (bottom), 90,
95, 99, 100, 101, 103. **NASA on The Commons @ Flickr
Commons:** cover (background), pp. 32 (bottom), 49. **Public
domain:** pp. 1, 5, 7, 13, 9, 15 (top), 29 (top and lower left),
30 (top, right center, left center), 32 (top), 33 (top, second
from top, bottom right), 42 (top), 48, 53 (top), 55, 56, 60,
61, 62 (middle), 63 (top), 67, 69, 70, 75 (top), 78 (bottom),
79 (top), 81, 84 (lower), 85 (both top), 89 (top), 92 (bottom),
93, 96, 102 (all except upper right, second from top).
Shutterstock: Steve Mann: p. 12 (top); Pete Spiro: p. 12
(second from top); paulinux: p. 12 (third from top); svlc:
p. 12 (bottom). **Wikipedia/Creative Commons:** Jdbrandt
at English Wikipedia: pp. 22–23; Science Museum (London):
p. 30 (bottom right); Thermos: p. 35; GeoffClarke: p. 92 (top);
WPPilot: p. 97; jaycarlcooper: p. 102 (upper right, second
from top). **Courtesy of Special Collections and Archives,
Wright State University:** pp. 8 (bottom), 10, 13 (bottom),
20 (right), 68 (bottom), 72 (top).

Publisher's note:
All quotations in this book come from original sources
and contain the spelling and grammatical inconsistencies of
the original text. Some of the quotations may also contain
terms that are no longer in use and may be considered
inappropriate or offensive. The use of such terms is for the
sake of preserving the historical and literary accuracy of the
sources and should not be seen as encouraging or endorsing
the use of such terms today.

Library and Archives Canada Cataloguing in Publication
Dakers, Diane, author
        Orville and Wilbur Wright : pioneers of the age of flight
/ Diane Dakers.
(Crabtree groundbreaker biographies)
Includes index.
Issued in print and electronic formats.
ISBN 978-0-7787-2609-8 (hardback).--ISBN 978-0-7787-2611-1
(paperback).--ISBN 978-1-4271-8103-9 (html)
        1. Wright, Orville, 1871-1948--Juvenile literature.
2. Wright, Wilbur, 1867-1912--Juvenile literature. 3. Inventors--
United States--Biography--Juvenile literature. 4. Aeronautics--
United States--Biography--Juvenile literature. 5. Aeronautics--
United States--History--Juvenile literature. I. Title.
II. Series: Crabtree groundbreaker biographies

TL540.W7D35 2016   j629.130092'2   C2016-904176-X
                                                  C2016-904177-8

Library of Congress Cataloging-in-Publication Data
Names: Dakers, Diane, author.
Title: Orville and Wilbur Wright : pioneers of the age of flight /
Diane Dakers.
Other titles: Crabtree groundbreaker biographies.
Description: St. Catharines, Ontario ; New York, NY : Crabtree
Publishing Company, [2017] | Series: Crabtree groundbreaker
biographies | Includes index.
Identifiers: LCCN 2016031766 (print) | LCCN 2016033051
(ebook) | ISBN 9780778726098 (reinforced library binding :
alk. paper) | ISBN 9780778726111 (pbk. : alk. paper) | ISBN
9781427181039 (Electronic HTML)
Subjects: LCSH: Wright, Orville, 1871-1948--Juvenile literature.
| Wright, Wilbur, 1867-1912--Juvenile literature. | Aeronautics-
-United States--Biography--Juvenile literature. | Aeronautics--
United States--History--20th century--Juvenile literature.
Classification: LCC TL540.W7 D35 2017 (print) | LCC TL540.W7
(ebook) | DDC 629.130092/273 [B] --dc23
LC record available at https://lccn.loc.gov/2016031766

Crabtree Publishing Company
www.crabtreebooks.com   1-800-387-7650

Printed in Canada/082016/TL20160715

Copyright © **2017 CRABTREE PUBLISHING COMPANY**. All rights reserved. No part of this
publication may be reproduced, stored in a retrieval system or be transmitted in any form or by
any means, electronic, mechanical, photocopying, recording, or otherwise, without the prior written
permission of Crabtree Publishing Company.

**Published
in Canada**
Crabtree Publishing
616 Welland Ave.
St. Catharines, Ontario
L2M 5V6

**Published in
the United States**
Crabtree Publishing
PMB16A
350 Fifth Ave., Suite 3308
New York, NY 10118

**Published in the
United Kingdom**
Crabtree Publishing
Maritime House
Basin Road North, Hove
BN41 1WR

**Published
in Australia**
Crabtree Publishing
3 Charles Street
Coburg North
VIC 3058

Contents

Chapter 1
Eyes on the Skies

A photographic illustration of Orville (left) and Wilbur Wright from a newspaper article published sometime after December 17, 1903, when the Wrights flew the first powered aircraft capable of controlled flight.

One day in 1878, a pair of young brothers eagerly awaited their father's return from a business trip. Their father was a church minister. He traveled often, serving a variety of communities throughout the American Midwest. When he came home from his trips, he always brought souvenirs and trinkets for his children—gifts designed to spark their imaginations and curiosity. Sometimes, the presents were as simple as a rock or other natural item. Sometimes, though, Milton Wright brought special treats. After this particular 1878 trip, the gift he brought for his sons, Wilbur and Orville, sent their imaginations soaring.

Born Inventors

Wilbur Wright was 11 years old, and his brother Orville was seven, the day their father

Opposite: Wilbur (shown left in posed photo) and Orville Wright often kept their pioneering work in aviation private. But they also thrilled crowds sometimes numbering in the thousands at public events and demonstrations. Images such as those shown here serve as a powerful reminder of the fact that every time the Wrights displayed their work to the public, people marveled at machines and feats that only a year or so earlier could only be imagined.

"Late in the autumn of 1878, our father came into the house one evening with some object partly concealed in his hands, and before we could see what it was, he tossed it into the air. Instead of falling to the floor, as we expected, it flew across the room till it struck the ceiling, where it fluttered awhile, and finally sank to the floor. It was a little toy, known to scientists as a 'hélicoptère.' ... A toy so delicate lasted only a short time in the hands of small boys, but its memory was abiding."

Orville Wright, *Century Magazine*, 1908

came home with a newfangled toy. It was a small flying gizmo, a sort of helicopter made of paper, bamboo, and cork. It had a rubber band connected to a propeller. The propeller was mounted atop of a stick. When the boys twirled the propeller with their fingers, the elastic wrapped tightly around the stick. When they let go, the elastic unwound quickly, spinning the propeller. The toy flew!

The little gadget was based on a design by Alphonse Pénaud, a French aviation pioneer. Alphonse had invented a "rubber torsion motor" in the early 1870s. Toymakers in Europe had been making miniature models of the device ever since—but the wonderful whirligig had only just made its way across the Atlantic Ocean to the United States.

Wilbur and Orville were fascinated with their new plaything. They called it a "bat."

THE BAT MAN

French inventor Alphonse Pénaud, the son of a navy admiral, was born in Paris in 1850. He intended to follow in his father's footsteps, but he had a hip condition that prevented him from joining the navy. Instead, the young man turned his interest in transportation to aircraft.

In 1870, Alphonse invented a rubber torsion motor—a motor operated by a twisted rubber band. Using this design, he built a model aircraft he called a "planophore." It was 20 inches (51 centimeters) long with an 18-inch (46-cm) wingspan. With its tail, rudder, and rear-mounted propeller, the planophore was the first model aircraft capable of stable (steady or secure) flight. It could fly almost 200 feet (60 meters).

Later, Alphonse built a small ornithopter, a flying machine that flapped its wings. He also created model helicopters. Toy versions of the helicopter and ornithopter were big sellers. It was one of the small helicopters that sparked the Wright brothers' interest in flying.

Throughout the 1870s, Alphonse experimented with different styles of wings, propellers, and landing gear. He eventually built full-sized flying machines. He even tested floating aircraft.

Many of Alphonse's ideas were sound, but so far ahead of their time that he was ridiculed for them. Because of that, and because nobody would help fund his projects, Alphonse gave up. He committed suicide in 1880 at age 30.

Today, he is considered one of the most important aviation pioneers of his time.

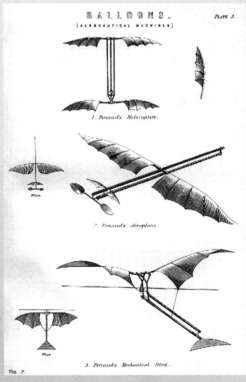

Three of Alphonse Pénaud's flying models. From top to bottom: the helicopter, the planophore (airplane), and the ornithopter.

The brothers played with the bat so much that they eventually broke it—but instead of crying over a wrecked toy, they built a new one. When that one wore out, they built another one. "We built a number of copies of the toy, which flew successfully," said Orville many years later.

Without even thinking about it, the young Wright brothers had built their first flying machine!

They didn't stop there, though. The inventive boys had so much fun building small bats that it gave them an idea for a bigger and better project. They set out to create a bat so big that the two of them could fly in it.

Orville and Wilbur tried a number of designs, using different combinations of materials, shapes, and concepts—but none of their supersized bats would fly. "We found that the larger the bat, the less it flew," said Orville.

Not surprisingly, the youngsters didn't yet know enough about the physics of flight to create a human-sized flying machine. "We finally became discouraged," said Orville. "We abandoned the experiments." Still, he said, that little bat was what launched the Wright brothers' future fascination with flight.

Taking Off

Unlike many parents of the day, Milton Wright and his wife Susan encouraged their kids to explore everything that grabbed their attention, to read as much as they could, and to let their imaginations soar. They wanted the kids to get outside, get dirty, build things, and broaden their horizons.

FLYING INTO HISTORY

The first person to design a workable flying machine was Leonardo da Vinci. In the 1480s, he came up with concepts for a number of aircraft, including the ornithopter, with its flapping wings, and his "aerial screw," an early helicopter. While da Vinci's machines never got off the ground, the Montgolfier brothers' hot-air balloon did. It took off for the first time in France in 1793.

In 1804, a British inventor flew a glider, an aircraft without an engine, for the first time. A German engineer improved on that design in 1891, creating a more practical glider. That same year, an American astronomer designed an airplane that used steam power, but it was too heavy to get off the ground.

After studying these previous designs, Orville and Wilbur Wright invented the first gasoline-powered airplane. The *Flyer*, as they called it, took off on December 17, 1903.

It's hard to say who invented the helicopter. Many people designed many different versions of it in the late 19th and early 20th centuries. The one that most closely resembles helicopters of today was invented in the United States in 1939 by a Russian-born engineer named Igor Sikorsky.

Leonardo da Vinci

A trading card shows the first public demonstration of the hot-air balloon designed and invented by the Montgolfier brothers, on June 4, 1783, in France.

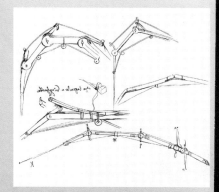

A detail from a diagram of one of Leonardo's flying machines, showing the flapping wings of an ornithopter.

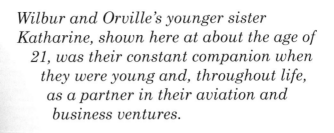

Wilbur and Orville's younger sister Katharine, shown here at about the age of 21, was their constant companion when they were young and, throughout life, as a partner in their aviation and business ventures.

Wilbur and Orville took that guidance to heart. Even though their life-sized flying machine hadn't worked out, the boys continued their childhood tinkering.

The introverted brothers were confident, determined, and mechanically gifted. They were also inseparable.

Because the Wright family moved often for Milton's work, the young, tight-knit twosome learned to depend on no one but each other and their family members. As children, the boys played together. As adults, they worked side by side on project after project. For most of their lives, they even lived in the same house—along with their younger sister Katharine, who worked with her brothers in their various business ventures. Neither brother ever married.

As Wilbur and Orville grew up, they never stopped inventing things—and reinventing themselves. When Orville was still a teenager, and with Wilbur barely in his 20s, they dove into the printing industry. When that company became successful, they moved into the bike business.

When that no longer posed a challenge to the creative brothers, they looked for a new direction in life. That new direction turned out

to be skyward.

At the time, in the mid-1890s, a number of international inventors were making news with their efforts to launch human flight. Orville and Wilbur—perhaps remembering how much fun they'd had with their bat years earlier—became fascinated with the idea of soaring like the birds.

They quietly jumped into the race to create a flying machine. After much trial, error, experimentation, and crash-landing, they figured it out. In 1903, Wilbur and Orville Wright invented the first powered aircraft capable of controlled flight.

It would be two years before they perfected it—and it would be a further three years before the international aviation community believed that the Wrights had actually flown.

When the world finally recognized Wilbur

Orville and Wilbur Wright took this photo of the Wright Flyer, *the first powered aircraft capable of controlled flight, sometime before their history-making flight on December 17, 1903.*

"It wasn't luck that made them fly. It was hard work and common sense. They put their whole heart and soul and all their energy into an idea and they had the faith."

John T. Daniels, one of five witnesses to the Wright brothers' first flight

and Orville as the inventors of the airplane, the brothers became global heroes—but it wasn't all smooth sailing. Competition from other aviators, near-fatal accidents, and years of legal battles drained the brothers' time, energy, and passion for flight. Claims that other aviators had invented human-powered flight before the Wright brothers created controversy in the aviation community for decades.

Today, however, Orville and Wilbur Wright are recognized as the fathers of flight. Every airplane that has been developed since 1903 uses the same basic building blocks the Wright brothers identified in 1903.

Until the Wright brothers put their minds to solving what they called "the flying problem," humans could only travel in two dimensions, moving across Earth's flat surface. Ultimately, these quiet, bookish, brilliant brothers solved the problem they'd set their minds to. They taught humans how to travel in an upward direction, a third dimension. They taught the world to fly.

For the past century, postal services around the world have issued dozens of stamps that pay tribute to the Wright brothers' contributions to flight.

A postcard, sent from France, featuring Orville (left) and Wilbur Wright, probably issued around 1908. After years of keeping their work secret, that was the year the brothers took both France and the United States by storm with spectacular public demonstrations of Flyer *planes.*

THE WRIGHT STUFF

In a 1908 article for *Century Magazine*, Orville Wright described for "the general reader" what it was like to fly a circle in a plane. Remember, only a handful of people had ever flown in an aircraft at this point in history:

"At a height of one hundred feet [30 m], you feel hardly any motion at all, except for the wind which strikes your face. If you did not take the precaution to fasten your hat before starting, you have probably lost it by this time. The operator moves a lever: the right wing rises, and the machine swings about to the left. You make a very short turn, yet you do not feel the sensation of being thrown from your seat, so often experienced in automobile and railway travel. You find yourself facing toward the point from which you started.... When you near the starting point, the operator stops the motor while still high in the air. The machine coasts down ... and comes to rest. Although the machine often lands when traveling at a speed of a mile a minute, you feel no shock whatever, and cannot, in fact, tell the exact moment at which it first touched the ground. The motor close beside you kept up an almost deafening roar during the whole flight, yet in your excitement, you did not notice it till it stopped."

Chapter 2
Bonded Brothers

Before they became known around the world as the celebrated, airplane-inventing "Wright Brothers," Orville and Wilbur were just two kids growing up in the Midwest. The boys were born four years apart, in two different towns, and had different dispositions—but they were so close, they might have been twins. Throughout their lives, this closeness became one of their secrets to success.

A Family on the Move

In 1859, Milton Wright, the son of a farmer, married Susan Koerner, the daughter of a carriage-maker. At 31 and 28, the newlyweds were considerably older than the typical bride and groom of the day. Still, the couple had

Below: a composite photo of images of Wilbur and Orville Wright's immediate family. Left to right: Wilbur Wright, Katharine Wright, Susan Koerner Wright, Lorin Wright, Milton Wright, Reuchlin Wright, and Orville Wright.

THE WRIGHT STUFF

The Wright family loved reading so much that the family home had two libraries in it. These rooms were filled with books about every subject imaginable—history, philosophy, theology (the study of religions), science, travel, genealogy, and language. Wilbur particularly enjoyed reading about history. The libraries also housed two complete sets of encyclopedias, collections of poetry, and works of fiction by the great writers of the day, such as Charles Dickens, Mark Twain, Sir Walter Scott, and Orville's favorite writer, Nathaniel Hawthorne, shown here as photographed by famed American photographer Matthew Brady between 1860 and 1865.

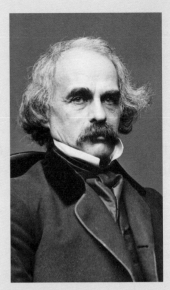

seven children together in the next 20 years.

Wilbur was the third child born in the family, and Orville was the sixth. They had two older brothers and a younger sister. A pair of twins, a girl and a boy born between Wilbur and Orville, died when they were just a few weeks old.

The Wright parents' late marriage was just one of the things that made the couple stand out at the time.

Susan was a rare young woman in that she was well educated. She graduated from high school and was a college student when she met her future husband. At the time, Milton was a preacher at the school where Susan studied. The pair bonded over a mutual love of learning. In particular, both shared an interest in literature and mathematics. Susan also loved sciences, while Milton pursued theology and languages.

Because of their own thirst for knowledge, Milton and Susan encouraged their children to read, explore a variety of interests, and study anything that struck their fancy.

Even more extraordinary for the era, Susan possessed a remarkable understanding of machinery. She had grown up helping her father in his carriage workshop and had inherited his knack for—and love of—all things mechanical. Over the years, Susan built such things as kitchen gadgets for the home, toys for the children, and a sled for outdoor fun.

She passed on her talent for tinkering to her kids, teaching them to build things, use tools, and understand how machinery worked.

Milton, on the other hand, wasn't at all technically inclined. Unlike some men of the era, though, he didn't object to Susan getting her hands dirty, and teaching the children to do the same.

Milton's position as a minister required that he move often to serve different communities

"We were lucky enough to grow up in a home environment where there was always much encouragement to children to pursue intellectual interests, to investigate whatever aroused curiosity. In a different kind of environment our curiosity might have been nipped long before it could have borne fruit."

Orville Wright

This house, at 7 Hawthorn Street in Dayton, Ohio, was the Wright family home from 1871 to 1914. Orville and Wilbur built the wraparound porch in the 1890s.

in the Midwest. Because of this, the five Wright children were born in four different towns in two different states. The eldest boys, Reuchlin and Lorin, were born in two different towns in Indiana. Wilbur was born in Millville, Indiana, on April 16, 1867.

Soon after Wilbur's birth, the Wrights moved to Dayton, Ohio, where they remained for the following eight years. Orville was born in a bedroom in the family's Dayton home on August 19, 1871. Little sister Katharine was born in the same room, on the same day, three years later.

When Milton was promoted to bishop of the Church of the United Brethren in 1877, the household was on the move again. For the next seven years, the family lived in at least three different homes in Indiana and Iowa, before returning to Dayton, for good, in 1884. By then

THE WRIGHT FAMILY'S CHURCH

Milton Wright was a minister, and later a bishop, with the Church of the United Brethren (UB).

This Anglican-based faith began informally in 1767 in Lancaster, Pennsylvania. It was officially organized and named in 1800. In the mid-1800s, the church opened colleges—to train ministers and to provide education for members of the public. Unlike other schools of the day, UB colleges welcomed women and people of color. Milton Wright, who had joined the church in 1846, met his wife, Susan, at one of these colleges.

Milton became a bishop in 1877, but lost the position four years later because of a conflict with church leaders. They wanted the church to become more liberal. Milton wanted to stick to the church's conservative roots.

Despite the disagreement, Milton was reelected as a bishop in 1885—but the conflict continued. In 1889, he split from the original church, establishing a new sect, the Church of the United Brethren (Old Constitution). About 10,000 followers (out of more than 200,000) joined him in this move.

Milton and his followers lost everything in the split. They had to start over, reorganize, and rebuild. Today, there are almost 500 Churches of the United Brethren around the world. All are descended from Bishop Wright's splinter group.

The liberal side of the original UB church eventually merged with the Methodist Church.

the Wrights had moved 12 times since Susan and Milton had married.

"As Inseparable as Twins"

Because the Wright family was always on the move, the children—especially the three youngest—became a tight-knit group. They learned to be self-sufficient, to rely on each other instead of outsiders.

Orville and Wilbur were particularly close. The brothers had the same interests, the same sense of curiosity, and the same passion for tinkering. They did everything together, and seemed to read each other's minds. They were "as inseparable as twins," said their father.

Because their parents encouraged the boys to explore, question, and learn, Wilbur and Orville became unusually independent—and a little mischievous.

As similar as they were, the brothers also had marked physical and personality differences. Wilbur was taller, thinner, and more athletic than his younger brother. He was serious and focused, often completely lost in thought. He was calm, intellectual, and a natural leader.

Wilbur in 1876, at around the age of nine.

Orville at around the age of five, in 1876.

Katharine Wright in 1879, at around the age of five.

> *"From the time we were little children, my brother Orville and myself lived together, played together, worked together and, in fact, thought together. We usually owned all of our toys in common, talked over our thoughts and aspirations, so that nearly everything that was done in our lives has been the result of conversations, suggestions, and discussions between us."*
>
> Wilbur Wright

Orville, on the other hand, was more impulsive. He was sensitive to criticism, full of ideas, and more easily distracted than Wilbur. At home, he was upbeat and entertaining, but he was painfully shy around strangers.

Both boys were self-confident and given to strong opinions. Not surprisingly, that could lead to terrible arguments between them!

One thing Orville and Wilbur always saw eye-to-eye on, though, was the need to build, to create, and to understand how mechanical things worked. They loved taking things apart and putting them back together.

That included rebuilding the toy helicopter, the "bat," that their father had brought them after one of his business trips. This gadget launched the boys' curiosity about flight, an interest that was revisited by Orville, the youngest Wright brother, a few years later.

When he was ten, Orville began designing and building kites. He felt he was too old to play with a kite by that age. Instead, he sold his creations to schoolmates to earn pocket money.

Meanwhile, one of Wilbur's earliest inventions was a machine for folding newspapers. He developed it while working with his father, who ran a church newspaper for many years. The device made the newspaper smaller and easier to mail.

Around the same time, the boys put their brains together to build a foot pedal-powered wood lathe to help speed up their wood-carving projects. Orville later said that this was their first partnership in a technical venture.

Death and New Life

In 1884, when the Wright family moved back to Dayton, Wilbur was in has final year of high school. Instead of enrolling in a Dayton school and graduating, he chose to work with his

father. Wilbur was such an excellent student that he knew he would be accepted at college, even without a high-school diploma.

He began taking courses to prepare himself for Yale University. He intended to study religion and become a minister, like his father.

That dream ended suddenly in 1886 when the 18-year-old was struck in the face with a hockey stick during an ice hockey game. The stick knocked out most of Wilbur's front teeth.

A panoramic view of Yale University, in New Haven, Connecticut. Wilbur's plans to attend Yale ended following a devastating hockey accident in 1886.

> *"She was of retiring disposition, very timid and averse to making any display in public, hence her true worth and highest qualities were most thoroughly appreciated by her family."*
>
> Obituary of Susan Wright, written by Wilbur and Orville

He suffered pain for months and wore false teeth for the rest of his life.

Eventually, his injuries healed, but the accident broke his spirit. Wilbur became quiet, withdrawn, and depressed. He gave up on his dream of attending college, and for three years, barely left the house. He spent his time reading and looking after his dying mother.

In the early 1880s, Susan Wright had contracted tuberculosis. Her health steadily declined for the next several years. After his accident, Wilbur became his mother's primary caregiver, until her death in July 1889. Susan was 58 years old when she died.

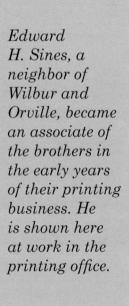

Edward H. Sines, a neighbor of Wilbur and Orville, became an associate of the brothers in the early years of their printing business. He is shown here at work in the printing office.

Just before his mother died, Orville also quit school. He was in his junior year of high school at the time. Like his elder brother, he never graduated. Unlike Wilbur, though, Orville had never been particularly academically inclined, or interested in school.

He was, however, interested in the printing business. He had been introduced to the industry by his father, who ran church newspapers throughout the boys' childhood.

In 1889, Orville opened his own print shop in Dayton, and soon Wilbur joined him in the business. A page from one of their first publications, the West Side News, *is shown here, with the brothers listed in the upper left corner as editor and publisher.*

Having spent two summers working as a printer's apprentice, 17-year-old Orville opened his own print shop in 1889. Wilbur soon joined him in the business. Together, the duo built the company's first printing press. At first, they ran the print shop out of a barn on the family property, but soon they were successful enough to open a storefront in downtown Dayton.

By then, the brothers had launched a weekly newspaper. The paper sold so well that, after a year, it became a daily publication. Unfortunately, competition was fierce in the news business at the time, with a dozen bigger papers already serving the city. The Wright brothers couldn't compete with those publications. They shut down their daily newspaper after just four months.

At that point, Wilbur and Orville decided to focus on printing other people's projects instead—such things as pamphlets, posters, advertisements, and business cards.

They also developed new technology for the printing industry and invented new types of printing presses.

The business, now called Wright & Wright, Job Printers, earned enough income to support the brothers financially. More importantly, perhaps, because of the advances they'd made in printing press technology, the young men were now known for their mechanical brilliance.

It wasn't long before Wilbur and Orville took those mechanical talents in a whole new direction. In the early 1890s, they became fascinated with a newfangled invention— the bicycle.

THE OTHER WRIGHT BROTHERS

Wilbur and Orville Wright had two older brothers—Reuchlin, born in 1861, and Lorin, born a year later. Neither of these two became as well-known as their younger siblings.

Reuchlin Wright was a wanderer. He attended college in Iowa, then Indiana, but graduated from neither school. After he married, he and his wife Lulu lived in Alabama, then Ohio and Missouri. Reuchlin and Lulu had four children. Eventually the family settled into life on a cattle farm in Kansas. Reuchlin died in 1920 at age 59.

After briefly living in Kansas and Indiana, Lorin Wright returned home to Dayton, Ohio. There, he married his high-school sweetheart, Ivonette, and had four children. Lorin worked for Wilbur and Orville in their print shop, and later ran the Wright Cycle Company with sister Katharine. Over the years, Lorin helped his younger brothers with their airplane experiments and tests. Later in life, he bought a toy company and manufactured a flying toy designed by Orville. Lorin died in 1939 at age 77.

Reuchlin Wright, shown here at about the age of 40 in 1901.

Lorin Wright, shown here in 1901 at about the age of 39, holding three of his children.

Chapter 3
The "Flying Problem"

The bicycle as we know it was invented in 1885 in England. By the early 1890s, bicycle fever had swept across the United States—and Wilbur and Orville Wright were caught up in the craze. The brothers bought bikes, joined a cycling club, and even entered a few races. They also became the go-to crew for cyclists who needed bike repairs. After all, everyone knew the Wright brothers were mechanical wizards! Business was so good that, in 1892, the Wrights hired a friend to run their printing company, and they opened a bicycle repair shop.

The Wright brothers at work in their bicycle repair shop, sometime around 1897. Left: Wilbur assembling parts. Right: Orville (thought to be on the left) and Edwin Sines, a neighbor and boyhood friend, filing bicycle frames.

Ground Transportation

A Laufmaschine (1817).

Inventors had been experimenting with two-wheeled modes of transport for centuries before a German fellow made a breakthrough in 1817. That year, Baron Karl von Drais invented the first human-powered, two-wheeled vehicle. The Laufmaschine, or running machine, looked like a bicycle, but it didn't have pedals. The rider powered it by walking or running, gathering enough speed to glide along the road.

For the next 40 years, designers around the world continued to experiment with two-, three-, and four-wheeled types of transport. They tested different types of mechanisms to power them.

In the 1860s, French inventors came up with the first two-wheel, pedal-powered vehicle, the "velocipede." A decade later came the "high-wheel bicycle," named for its huge front wheel.

A velocipede (1868).

A high-wheel bicycle (1880).

This bike had wire spokes and rubber tires. The big front wheel meant a rider could travel farther with one push of the pedal—but it also meant the bicycle was difficult, and often dangerous, to ride.

In 1885, an Englishman named John Kemp Starely came up with the "safety bicycle." With its same-sized wheels, and chain-and-gear mechanism, this design remains the basis for bicycles today.

With a few design improvements, this machine launched a worldwide bicycle craze—something that sparked the imaginations of Orville and Wilbur Wright.

A safety bicycle (1885).

Looking to the Skies

Not content to merely *repair* bicycles, Orville and Wilbur soon began manufacturing them. They custom-made every bike for the individual who bought it. Naturally, the more bikes they built, the more improvements the inventive brothers added to the original design. They also handcrafted bicycle parts and invented machines to speed up the construction process.

By 1896, the Wright Cycle Company was a booming business. Having mastered the bike-building biz, the Wright brothers started seeking a new challenge.

That summer, reports of inventors around the world testing flying machines filled newspapers. A fellow named Otto Lilienthal, also called "the Flying Man," was the most famous of them all.

"In 1896, we read ... of the experiments of Otto Lilienthal, who was making gliding flights from the top of a small hill in Germany," said Orville. Sadly, Lilienthal crashed one of his gliders and died that same summer. "His death ... increased our interest in the subject, and we began looking for books pertaining to flight."

Wilbur and Orville couldn't get enough information on the subject. The idea of human flight, something most people dismissed as impossible, fascinated the brothers.

"Thousands of the most dissimilar body structures—such as insects, reptiles, birds, and mammals—were flying every day at pleasure," said Wilbur. "[So] it was reasonable to suppose that man might also fly."

In 1896, the year Lilienthal crashed his glider and died, an American scientist named Samuel Pierpont Langley launched his own version of a flying machine. He called it the *Aerodrome*. After many tries, Langley's unpiloted mini-airplane flew for 90 seconds. Six months later, it managed to stay in the air almost two minutes—long enough to fly 4,800 feet (1,460 m). Langley's work so impressed the U.S. government that the U.S. Army gave him $50,000 (a fortune at the time) to continue his *Aerodrome* experiments.

A portrait from 1864–1865 of American astronomer, physicist, and inventor Samuel Pierpont Langley.

THE SUMMER OF 1896

Orville and Wilbur Wright weren't the first people to focus their minds on "the flying problem." A number of aviation pioneers had come before them—and provided inspiration and information that helped the brothers learn to fly. The summer of 1896 was a turning point in aviation history.

- Samuel Pierpont Langley, a well-known American astronomer, began his studies of flight in 1886. He designed an unmanned aircraft called the *Aerodrome*. In May 1896, after years of testing and modifying the *Aerodrome*, the craft took flight. It soared for about 90 seconds. Samuel made a few more flights in November 1896, before taking a three-year break from his flight studies.

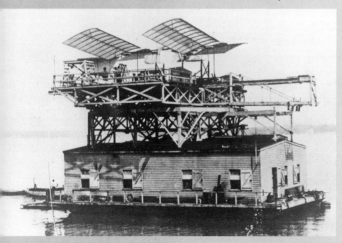

The Langley Aerodrome, *shown above a launching structure in 1903, just moments before attempting a manned flight that ended when the craft fell into the Potomac River in Washington, D.C.*

At the same time, another American, Octave Chanute, was experimenting with *manned* gliders and aircraft.

Despite the limited success of these aviators, their work inspired Orville and Wilbur.

For the next few years, the brothers turned their mechanical minds to the "flying problem," as they called it. They devoured every book,

German engineer and aviation pioneer Otto Lilienthal, photographed around 1896.

- German engineer Otto Lilienthal and his brother Gustav began studying flight in the 1860s. Otto wrote a book and many articles about their groundbreaking research in aerodynamics. Beginning in 1890, Otto made more than 2,000 test flights in 16 different styles of glider. He died after a glider crash in August 1896. His last words were reported to be "Sacrifices must be made."

- In 1894, American engineer Octave Chanute published a book called *Progress in Flying Machines*. Then he set out to invent one. Using Otto Lilienthal's research as a starting point, Octave and his colleague, Augustus Herring, began testing their own glider designs in the summer of 1896. In August, a few weeks after Otto's death, they made a series of short flights. At that point, the Chanute-Herring glider was the most advanced aircraft in the world.

Below: The glider that took the life of its inventor, Otto Lilienthal, following its crash in 1896.

Below: A model of a craft known as Octave Chanute's Glider Triplane.

French-born American civil engineer and aviation pioneer Octave Chanute.

Below: American aviation pioneer Augustus Herring in one of his early gliders, around 1894.

The Wright Stuff

To further his understanding of the subject, Wilbur wrote to the Smithsonian Institution, in Washington, D.C., the world's largest museum and research complex, asking for information about flight. Here is an excerpt from his letter, dated May 30, 1899:

"I am about to begin a systematic study of the subject in preparation for practical work to which I expect to devote what time I can spare from my regular business. I wish to obtain such papers as the Smithsonian Institution has published on this subject, and if possible, a list of other works in print in the English language. I am an enthusiast, but not a crank in the sense that I have some pet theories as to the proper construction of a flying machine. I wish to avail myself of all that is already known and then if possible add my mite to help on the future worker who will attain final success."

report, and news article they could find about flying and experiments relating to human-powered flight.

Through their studies, they quickly figured out that the secret to flying an aircraft wasn't about power. It was about the ability to control the flying machine. They believed that the reason previous flight experiments had failed was because the pilots could not raise, lower, or turn their aircraft. They were at the mercy of the winds.

Next, the brothers studied birds in flight. They paid particular attention to the structure and movements of avian wings. They observed that birds tilted their bodies slightly, and shifted certain wing feathers, to make a mid-flight direction change. Wilbur noticed that a bird "presents one [wing] tip at a positive angle and the other at a negative angle … turning itself into an animated windmill, and that when its body had revolved as far as it wished, it reversed the process."

Unlike other aviators, the Wrights realized that air travel was not a two-dimensional activity, like riding a bike on a road, or moving a boat across water. Flying an aircraft was a three-dimensional pursuit.

An aircraft needed to tilt like a bird did, when it was time to turn. It needed to move up and down through the air. The flying machine's side-to-side movement also had to be controllable.

The Wright brothers were the first to recognize these three elements as the keys to creating a machine capable of safe flight. Armed with this new understanding, the inventive young men put their mechanical know-how to work.

> *"We could not understand that there was anything about a bird that would enable it to fly that could not be built on a larger scale and used by man."*
>
> Orville Wright

One key principle of aviation that the Wright brothers grasped was that aircraft needed to tilt in order to turn, like this jackdaw in flight.

THE FLYING SOLUTIONS

The Wrights knew that in addition to power and wings, the key to flight was in the pilot's ability to control the craft. To develop this, they looked at each element of the aircraft individually.

- **Wings:** An aircraft's wings serve two main purposes—keeping the plane in the air and allowing it to tilt, or **roll**, which is essential to turning in the air (diagram below). Having observed birds in flight, the Wrights knew that, for an aircraft to turn, its wings had to be able to "warp," as they called it. That meant one wing would twist up, while the other twisted down, forcing the plane into a turn. The brothers developed a system of cables attached to the wing tips so the pilot could control the turns. They also found that wings with a curved surface had more lift, the force that holds the plane in the air. They experimented with 200 different wing designs to find the best combination of wingspan (length of the wings from wing tip to wing tip), camber (curve), and chord (width of wing).

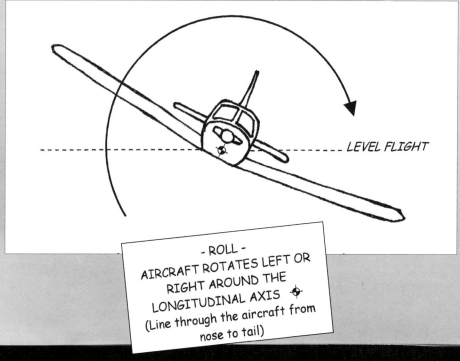

LEVEL FLIGHT

- ROLL -
AIRCRAFT ROTATES LEFT OR RIGHT AROUND THE LONGITUDINAL AXIS
(Line through the aircraft from nose to tail)

- **Elevator:** The elevator is the device that controls a plane's **pitch**, its up-and-down movement in the air (diagram right). The Wright brothers mounted the elevator at the front of the plane. They believed this would give them more control over the craft's pitch, and prevent the plane from nose-diving. Having the elevator at the front means the pilot can move the nose of the plane up and down quickly. It also means the plane might move up and down too quickly, causing instability. Today, the elevator is usually located in the rear of an aircraft to allow for greater pitch control.

FLIGHT PATH

- PITCH -
AIRCRAFT ROTATES UP OR DOWN AROUND THE HORIZONTAL AXIS
(Horizontal line through the center of the aircraft from wingtip to wingtip)

- **Rudder:** A plane's rudder, or moveable tail, helps prevent the craft from slipping sideways, or **yawing**, in the air (diagram below). Although the Wrights didn't think a flying machine needed a tail, they added a horizontal one (like a bird's tail) to give the plane more surface area. They soon realized a vertical tail would provide side-to-side stability. The fixed vertical tail helped, but they still struggled to maintain control in the air. The brothers soon had a brainstorm to solve this problem. They realized that, when the wings warped to make a turn, the force of the air on the raised wing caused that side of the plane to slow down slightly. This, in turn, caused the plane to slip sideways. They discovered that, by moving the tail to one side or the other, it reduced this motion and kept the plane flying straight.

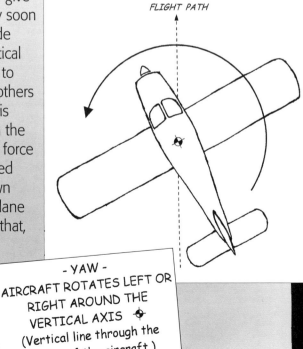

FLIGHT PATH

- YAW -
AIRCRAFT ROTATES LEFT OR RIGHT AROUND THE VERTICAL AXIS
(Vertical line through the center of the aircraft)

Testing, Testing

By the end of the 19th century, the bicycle market was no longer profitable. The industry was flooded with companies manufacturing the two-wheeled mode of transport. By this time, too, the U.S. Army was funding the Wrights' competitor, Samuel Langley, in his flight research. Wilbur and Orville realized that there was no more money to be made in the bike business—their financial future was in aircraft!

They left the Wright Cycle Company in the hands of their brother Lorin and sister Katharine, and turned their focus to figuring out how to fly.

The brothers began experimenting with the three elements they had identified as crucial to safe flight—the ability to tilt a flying machine (roll), to move it up and down through the air (pitch), and to control its side-to-side movements (yaw).

After a year of experimenting and testing theories on kites, the Wrights were ready to take their ideas to the skies. Using one of their kite designs as a model, they built a glider big enough to carry a pilot. The lightweight wood

"[The glider] is not to have a motor and is not expected to fly in any true sense. My idea is merely to experiment and practice with a view of solving the problem of equilibrium.... In my experiments, I do not expect to rise many feet from the ground, and in case I am upset, there is nothing but soft sand to strike on."

Wilbur Wright, in a letter to his father, 1900

frame had a 17-foot (5.2-m) wingspan. Wilbur, an expert at sewing, made wing coverings out of cotton fabric.

The brothers identified Kitty Hawk, a village on the North Carolina coast, as the perfect place to conduct their first flight tests. It was windy enough to give lift to the glider's wings. It was sparsely populated, so the brothers could experiment in secret. It also had miles of wide-open sandy beaches that would provide a soft landing when the glider crashed—and no doubt it would crash!

In the autumn of 1900, the brothers shipped their glider 700 miles (1,130 kilometers) southeast from Dayton to Kitty Hawk. Just south of the village of Kitty Hawk was a collection of high sand dunes called Kill Devil Hills. This would be the site of the brothers' flight tests for the next three years.

At first, the Wrights flew the glider as an unmanned kite—to see how the control systems operated at the windy site. Soon, Wilbur climbed aboard. He lay flat, or prone, between the bottom wings.

Wilbur (left) and Orville Wright test their glider as an unmanned kite in 1900.

On October 20, 1900, he made about a dozen glides in the craft. Each voyage lasted just 15 or 20 seconds and traveled only a few hundred feet. Still, it was cause for the brothers to cheer. Said Wilbur:

"We were very much pleased with the general results. With an entirely untried form of machine, we considered it quite a point to be able to return [home] without having our pet theories completely knocked in the head ... and our own brains dashed out in the bargain."

Before the Wrights left Kitty Hawk on October 23, a strong wind picked up the glider and dashed it into the ground. It was destroyed, but the brothers were finished with it anyway. They returned to Dayton—and to the drawing board—to redesign and rebuild their aircraft.

The following summer, Orville and Wilbur experimented at Kitty Hawk with a new glider. This one had larger wings and a modified control system. Wilbur again conducted a number of short flights. This time, though, the craft was "less manageable than expected," he said. It stalled and crashed over and over again.

The young men, now in their early 30s, made a number of changes to the machine. A week later, when Wilbur took off again, the glider flew a record

Battered by strong winds, the Wright brothers' glider lies in a heap at Kitty Hawk, just a few days before they returned to Dayton in October 1900.

distance—386 feet (118 m)—but it barely cleared the ground.

There was another, more serious, problem. Every time Wilbur attempted a turn in the aircraft, it would swing in the wrong direction or spin out of control. The plane seemed to have a mind of its own.

After one particularly spectacular crash, in which Wilbur was seriously injured and the glider seriously damaged, the brothers gave up and headed back to Dayton.

They felt they had failed. "We doubted that we would ever resume our experiments," Wilbur said. "At this time, I made the prediction that man would sometime fly, but that it would not be in our lifetime."

Taking Flight

Despite their frustration with their 1901 flight attempts, Wilbur and Orville weren't the kind of people to give up on anything. In late 1901, they resumed their efforts to solve the flying problem.

Wilbur lies prone just after his 1901 glider comes to a stop in the sand at Kitty Hawk, North Carolina. Skid marks from the landing are visible behind the craft.

In 1901, the Wrights returned to Dayton, frustrated in their attempts to control their glider at Kitty Hawk. Back home, they built this wind tunnel in their bicycle shop and tested hundreds of wing shapes in order to come up with a more effective wing design.

They constructed a wind tunnel at their Dayton bicycle workshop (which was now also their aircraft workshop). They designed, built, and tested about 200 different wing styles, until they found the ones that worked best in the wind tunnel. The brothers discovered that longer, narrower, flatter wings worked better than the chunky-style wings they had mounted on their first two gliders.

The following summer, in 1902, Wilbur and Orville returned to Kitty Hawk with yet another glider. This one was a biplane, with streamlined, double-decker wings measuring 32 feet (10 m) from tip to tip. The improved wings allowed the aircraft to make longer, more stable flights.

The kitchen of the Wright brothers' camp at Kitty Hawk was neatly arranged with shelves holding dishes, canned foods, and cooking utensils.

This glider also had a new mechanism—a tail with a pair of vertical fins. The Wrights hoped the tail would help control the craft's out-of-control turns. Most of the time it did. Occasionally, though, the glider still spun wildly when the pilot brought the craft out of a turn. Orville realized that the tail needed to be able to move, like a bird's tail, to stabilize the plane in certain wind conditions.

"With this improvement, our serious troubles ended," said Wilbur. "Thereafter, we devoted ourselves to the work of gaining skill by continued practice."

With the success of their 1902 glider, the Wright brothers had invented the first aircraft capable of fully controlled flight! The craft had wings that could twist, to allow the plane to roll—and therefore turn. The tail, or rudder, helped control the side-to-side sliding motion, or yaw. An elevator, mounted at the front of the plane, allowed the pilot to raise or lower the nose of the craft.

Wings

Elevator

Rudder

Wilbur makes a right turn in the Wright brothers' 1902 biplane glider. This photo illustrates some of the key principles and mechanics of controlled flight. The wings are able to "warp," or twist up and down, to allow the plane to roll, which is essential to turning. The rudder, or tail, which is the vertical piece in the back, helps control side-to-side motion, or yaw. And the device known as the elevator, a horizontal piece at the front, allows the pilot to control the pitch, or raising and lowering of the nose of the craft. Today, most planes' elevators are located at the rear, and they are similar to the flaps that move up and down on the main wings of the plane.

In the fall of 1902, the brothers made hundreds of controlled test flights in their new glider. As word got out, many people, including fellow aviator Octave Chanute, arrived at Kitty Hawk to watch history in the making. As Orville wrote after one particularly great day of flying:

"We now hold all the records. The largest machine ever handled, the longest distance glide (American), the longest time in the air, the smallest angle of descent, and the highest wind!!!"

THE WRIGHT STUFF

In March 1903, the Wright brothers applied for a patent for a "Flying Machine," based on their 1902 glider design. Some aviation historians believe that the brothers' 1902 glider—with its three-axis flight control—marked the invention of the airplane.

These drawings were typical of the patent plans submitted by the Wrights for their "Flying Machine." Shown here is a set of plans for a Flyer *identified as a "Wright brothers aeroplane."*

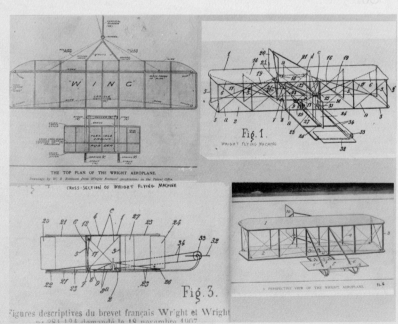

When the Wright brothers returned to Dayton in October 1902, they were flying high with excitement. They knew they were now at the front of the pack in the race to develop the world's first powered flying machine. "Before leaving [Kitty Hawk]," said Orville, "we were already at work on the general design of a new machine which we proposed to propel with a motor."

Flying High

Orville and Wilbur spent the next year experimenting with different types of propellers, wings, and materials for their new, powered aircraft. They also searched for a company to make an engine that would be lightweight, but powerful enough for flight. Every engine manufacturer they asked said it couldn't be done—so the brothers built an engine themselves, with the help of Wright Cycle Company bicycle mechanic Charlie Taylor.

The Wrights called their airplane-in-progress the *Flyer*. It was a biplane with a wingspan of 40 feet (12 m). It was made of spruce, a lightweight wood, with cotton fabric covering the wings, rudder, and elevator. It featured two 8-foot (2.4 m), hand-carved propellers.

Inventor and mechanic Charlie Taylor. Orville and Wilbur initially hired Charlie to fix bicycles in their repair shop. He eventually assisted in running the shop while the Wrights developed and flew gliders. When the Wrights began work on their motorized Flyer *craft, the brothers turned to him to take their rough sketches and create the plane's engine.*

In September 1903, the Wright brothers shipped the *Flyer* to Kill Devil Hills for its first test flights. Problems with the propellers and frigid, windy weather slowed their progress. Finally, on December 14, the *Flyer* was ready to go. Wilbur and Orville flipped a coin to decide who would make the first flight. Wilbur won. He lay down between the *Flyer*'s bottom wings, took off, and … crashed into the sand.

The flight had lasted three-and-a-half seconds.

After repairing the *Flyer*, it was now Orville's turn to try. On December 17, 1903, just after 10:30 in the morning, he climbed in, took off, and flew! The flight only lasted 12 seconds and traveled just 120 feet (37 m)—but, as Wilbur said:

> *"[I]t was the first [flight] in the history of the world in which a machine carrying a man had raised itself by its own power into the air in full flight, had sailed forward without reduction of speed, and had finally landed at a point as high as that from which it had started."*

Members of the Wrights' support crew (accompanied by two small boys and a dog), help move the Flyer *to its launching track on the Kill Devil Hills sand dunes at Kitty Hawk. This picture was taken just before the failed trial flight on December 14, 1903.*

December 17, 1903: In this famous photo, Orville is at the controls of the Flyer, *lying prone, and Wilbur has just released the right wing of the plane after running alongside to steady it. At this moment, the Wright brothers have become the first humans in history to complete a sustained, controlled, powered, heavier-than-air flight. Orville set up the camera ahead of time and had one of the witnesses to the event, John Daniels, squeeze the rubber bulb at the moment Wilbur let go of the wing and stood aside. The photo itself has become a classic and is one of the most recognized pieces of photography to come out of the 20th century.*

Five Kitty Hawk villagers witnessed the historic first flight. One of them, John Daniels, snapped a now-famous photograph of the event. In an interview years later, John said the *Flyer* was "as pretty as any bird you ever laid your eyes on. I don't think I ever saw a prettier sight in my life."

After that famous first takeoff, the Wright brothers took turns and made three more flights that day. The longest one, piloted by Wilbur

"Success. Four flights Thursday morning all against twenty-one mile [34 km] wind. Started from level with engine power alone. Average speed through the air thirty-one miles [50 km]. Longest 57 seconds. Inform press. Home Christmas."

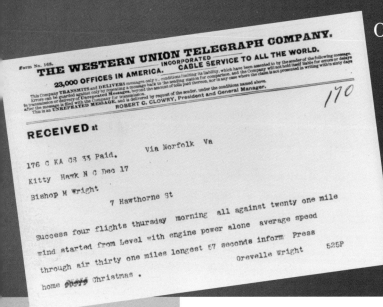

Orville Wright's telegram to his father Milton, informing him of four successful flights on December 17, 1903 (Note: The person transmitting the telegram erroneously spelled Orville's name "Orvelle" and wrote "57 seconds" instead of "59 seconds.")

around noon, covered 852 feet (260 m) in 59 seconds.

As they prepared for a fifth flight, a wind gust flipped the *Flyer* over, damaging it beyond repair. The *Flyer* never flew again.

Even though the Wright brothers had just become the first humans in history to complete a sustained, controlled, powered flight, their feat didn't cause much of a stir. Some people felt the flights were too short to count. Others were convinced flight was impossible, so the brothers' claim to have flown could not be true. The only newspaper that covered the story, the *Virginian-Pilot*, wrote such a ridiculous—and mostly made up—account of the flights that it only added to the disbelief.

The Wrights submitted their own account of their December 17 activities to newspapers, but nobody paid attention.

Back to the Drawing Board

In 1904, to save money, and so they could work on their aircraft year-round, the Wright brothers moved their flight-testing center closer to home. They leased a field called Huffman Prairie, just outside Dayton. There, they erected a hangar, where they rebuilt the *Flyer*, with a few modifications.

On May 23, 1904, the brothers invited reporters and photographers to Huffman Prairie to watch a demonstration of the newly built *Wright Flyer II*. About 40 people showed up to see the flight. Unfortunately, the brothers couldn't get the plane off the ground that day.

Orville (left) and Wilbur stand alongside the Flyer II *outside its hangar at Huffman Prairie in May 1904. The brothers had recently returned to Dayton to continue working on their designs closer to home.*

This photograph, taken in 1905, is the first to show the Wright brothers' catapult launching device (structure shown at right). Here, Orville is at the controls, and the two figures in the center are thought to be Wilbur and Charlie Taylor, who helped build and maintain the Flyer engines.

After another failed demo two days later, reporters lost interest, and the Wright brothers went back to the drawing board.

They soon figured out that, without the strong winds of Kitty Hawk, the *Flyer II* didn't have enough lift to take off. To help the plane become airborne, the inventor brothers built a catapult to fling the craft forward with enough speed that it could take to the sky.

The system worked. By mid-September 1904, the Wrights spent more and more time in the air in the *Flyer II*. On September 20, Wilbur flew the first complete circle in the air in history. The only person on hand to witness the event was a beekeeper named Amos Root. He'd heard rumors of the Wrights' flying machine and had driven miles to see it in person. Amos wrote about the circular flight for a small beekeeping journal. "When it turned that circle and came near the starting point, I was right in front of it," he wrote in *Gleanings in Bee Culture*. "It was the grandest sight of my life."

By the end of 1904, the Wright brothers had made more than 100 flights in the *Flyer II*. Still, the aircraft was unstable. It crashed often—so they rebuilt it yet again.

The Wrights launched the *Flyer III* in June 1905. A month later, it crashed, almost killing

In September 1905, with Orville at the controls, the *Flyer III makes two complete circles of the field at Huffman Prairie in under three minutes.*

Wilbur—but the brothers refused to give up. They spent the next two months modifying the *Flyer III* and, come fall, they had pretty much perfected it.

In September 1905, the Wright brothers made longer and longer flights. On October 5, the *Flyer III* made a 24-mile (39-km) flight, staying in the air for an astounding 38 minutes. The flight only ended because the aircraft ran out of gas. It coasted to a safe landing.

Of course, you can't fly the world's first aircraft for 38 minutes without your neighbors noticing.

The following day, reporters and photographers showed up at the airfield asking for a demonstration. This time, the Wright brothers refused. They knew they had invented the world's first practical aircraft—and they knew they could make money with it. They feared that, if photos got out, other inventors would steal their ideas.

The Wrights decided they would not fly again until someone agreed to buy and manufacture the airplane. That resolution would keep them grounded for almost three years.

"Our 1905 improvements have given such results as to justify the assertion that flying has been transformed from the realm of scientific problems to that of useful arts."

Wilbur Wright

Chapter 4
Flying High on Fame and Fortune

Orville and Wilbur Wright did not make a single flight in 1906 or 1907. Instead, they spent their time trying to sell their history-making flying machine. The first organization they approached was the U.S. military. It was logical, they thought, that the U.S. Army be the first to own a *Wright Flyer III*. The government didn't see it that way. Two different military departments turned the Wrights down. The brothers then set their sights on France, a nation of aviation enthusiasts. The French government also refused to buy a Wright aircraft. Germany and England also said no. The problem was, of course, that nobody wanted to buy a plane without seeing a demonstration—how could a buyer be certain the thing could actually fly?

The early Flyer *planes had two sets of rudders—double horizontal rudders in the front and double vertical rudders in the rear. In this photo, the plane is flying toward the right of the picture.*

THE WRIGHT STUFF

When the Wrights made their first famous flight, in 1903, future politician James M. Cox was publisher of the *Dayton Daily News*. Years later, he defended his newspaper's lack of coverage of the historic event. "Frankly, none of us believed it," he said.

Let's Make a Deal

Because Wilbur and Orville were so secretive about the *Wright Flyer III*, nothing appeared in newspapers about their groundbreaking work. The lack of photographs and press reports led the international aviation community to question whether the brothers had really designed and flown an aircraft at all. After all, if they had done this amazing thing, wouldn't the local media have let the world know about it?

French aviators, who vowed they would be the first to fly, were particularly scornful of the Wrights' work. They called the brothers *bluffeurs* (bluffers). In February 1906, the Paris edition of the *New York Herald* summed up popular opinion about the Wright brothers. Were they "fliers or liars," it asked.

Early in 1906, things finally started turning around for Wilbur and Orville.

After conducting an investigation, the Aero Club of America announced that it believed the Wrights had, in fact, invented the world's first airplane. The organization publicly congratulated the brothers for "devising,

> *"The Wrights have flown or they have not flown. They possess a machine or they do not possess one. They are in fact either fliers or liars. It is difficult to fly. It's easy to say 'We have flown.'"*
>
> The *New York Herald*, Paris edition, February 1906

constructing, and operating a successful, man-carrying dynamic flying machine."

The Aero Club's acknowledgment inspired *Scientific American* magazine to also review the Wrights' claims. In April 1906, the magazine wrote: "There is no doubt whatever that these able experimenters deserve the highest credit for having perfected the first flying machine ... which has ever flown successfully and at the same time carried a man."

Six weeks later, in May 1906, more good news came for Orville and Wilbur. The U.S. Patent Office finally granted them a patent for their 1902 "Flying Machine." It had been three years since they had first applied for legal protection for their work. The patent meant the brothers could at last demonstrate the *Flyer III* in public, without fear of someone stealing their ideas.

Still, it would be another two years of letters, telegrams, political maneuvering, meetings—and frustrations—before the Wrights sold an aircraft.

This certificate, issued by the U.S. Patent Office on May 22, 1906, grants the Wright brothers a patent for "an alleged new and useful improvement in Flying Machines."

In the spring of 1907, the U.S. Army finally agreed to consider buying a two-seat *Wright Flyer III*. The French government showed interest shortly after. Both parties wanted demonstrations of the aircraft before finalizing any deal.

Orville and Wilbur immediately began building a number of new airplanes to present to their potential buyers. Before long, though, the American and French deals got so bogged down in political complications that it looked like neither would happen after all.

In desperation, Orville and Wilbur traveled to France with one of their aircraft in the summer of 1907. They hoped to convince the French government to honor its agreement to buy a plane.

While they were in France, the Wrights happened to meet an officer in the Aeronautical Division of the U.S. Army. Lieutenant Frank Lahm believed in the brothers. He wrote to his commander that he considered it "unfortunate that this American invention, which unquestionably has considerable military value, should not be first acquired by the United States Army."

Army officer Frank Lahm met the Wright brothers on August 1, 1907, the very same day that the Army's Aeronautical Division was created. That meeting led to a lifelong friendship. It also convinced him to champion the brothers' cause with the U.S. Army. Frank would eventually become a Wright-trained aviator, and in 1909 he became the military's first certified pilot.

Immediately, the army invited Wilbur and Orville to meet members of the military upon their return to the United States. That meeting happened in New York City on November 25, 1907.

A few months later, the Wright brothers' years of effort finally paid off. Early in 1908, the U.S. government agreed to buy one of their planes. The army wanted an aircraft that could seat a pilot and passenger, travel 125 miles (200 km) at a speed of 40 miles (65 km) per hour, and stay aloft for at least an hour. It also had to be easy enough to fly that "an intelligent man" could learn to do it.

Within weeks of signing the contract with the U.S. government, the good news continued for the brothers. In March, a group of French investors agreed to purchase Wright planes to sell in France.

A close-up view of the Flyer III *showing its design for military use. The U.S. government specified that the craft have two seats, one for the pilot and another for a passenger.*

To finalize the two deals, Wilbur and Orville still had to demonstrate that their aircraft could fly. They split up to present their flying machines on opposite sides of the Atlantic Ocean. Wilbur sailed for Europe to work with the French group, while Orville stayed in the United States to work with the Americans.

Showing the World How to Fly

Before they left for their respective sales presentations, Orville and Wilbur had to relearn how to fly. After all, it had been more than two and a half years since either of them had piloted the *Flyer III*.

They couldn't practice in Dayton. Now that the word was out that they had signed a deal with the U.S. government, they were famous. Reporters, photographers, and fans followed the Wrights everywhere they went.

In April 1908, the brothers decided to return to secluded Kitty Hawk to practice in private. Of course, they didn't find privacy or solitude there, either. When word got out that the Wrights were flying at Kitty Hawk, the press flocked there to witness the first flights of the new aircraft—a two-seat, modified version of the *Wright Flyer III*. The new plane was called the *Wright Model A Flyer*.

At first, the brothers flew with sandbags in the passenger seat to get used to carrying extra weight. On May 14, 1908, Wilbur finally took a guest for a ride. That day, a friend named Charlie Furnas became the first airplane passenger in history!

Having refreshed their own skills, the brothers set out to show the world how to fly.

At the end of May, Wilbur traveled to France to demonstrate the *Model A Flyer* to the French buyers. He chose a horse-racing course near Le Mans, about 125 miles (200 km) southwest of Paris, as his flight center.

Before he could take off, though, Wilbur had to repair the plane he and Orville had shipped to France a year earlier. It had been badly damaged during transit. It took two months for Wilbur and a crew of local mechanics to fix it.

As the plane shaped up, local residents began showing up at the racecourse to watch Wilbur's progress. That meant a number of people—including famous French fliers Louis Blériot and Ernest Archdeacon—were on hand on August 8, when Wilbur took his first flight tests at the racetrack. Even though Wilbur only flew two circles in the sky, and was only airborne for two minutes, the crowd was stunned. "*Il vole!*" cried a small boy as he ran to tell the townspeople. "He flies!"

Wilbur adjusts the engine of the Model A Flyer *in Le Mans, France. The plane had been so badly damaged during shipment from the United States that it needed to be rebuilt.*

*A French
publication
celebrates
Wilbur Wright's
flight of the
Model A Flyer
at a racetrack
near Le Mans,
France, on
August 8,
1908. Roughly
translated,
the headline
proclaims,
"W. Wright
Has Flown!"*

W. WRIGHT A VOLÉ!

PREMIER ESSAI, PREMIER SUCCÈS

Wilbur Wright a couvert, en son premier essai, plus de 2 kilomètres, à une vitesse de 65 kilomètres à l'heure et à 15 mètres de hauteur. — L'enthousiasme au Mans.

"*C'est merveilleux*," said Blériot. "It's marvelous."

Wilbur made another eight, more technically challenging, flights during the following week, wowing the public, the media, and fellow aviators with his flying displays. Thousands of onlookers flocked to airfields to watch him soar.

Immediately, Wilbur was front-page news across Europe. "I have today seen Wilbur Wright and his great white bird, the beautiful mechanical bird," wrote a reporter for *Le Figaro*. "There is not a doubt. Wilbur and Orville Wright have well and truly flown."

Another reporter for a different newspaper wrote: "Not one of the former detractors of the Wrights dare question, today, the previous experiments of the men who were truly the first to fly."

Even Ernest Archdeacon, who had been one of the Wright brothers' greatest critics, had to admit he'd been wrong about their abilities. "For too long a time, the Wright brothers have been accused in Europe of bluffing," he wrote.

"They are today hallowed [worshiped] in France, and I feel an intense pleasure in counting myself among the first to make amends for that flagrant injustice."

Even when Wilbur crashed the plane on August 13, 1908, fans were thrilled. "Mr. Wright is as superb in his accidents as he is in his flight," said a French aircraft designer, as quoted in the *New York Herald*.

The people of Le Mans showered Wilbur with food and gifts, flowers and fruit baskets. A musician wrote a song about him. A colleague at the racetrack adopted a stray dog and called him Flyer.

By the time Wilbur returned to the skies a week after his crash, admirers were arriving by the trainload to watch the flying machine in motion.

The Wright brothers had finally proved themselves in Europe. The French newspapers

French flier Ernest Archdeacon, once suspicious of reports of the Wright brothers' achievements, became a supporter when he witnessed the performance of the Model A Flyer *in France.*

> *"All question as to who originated the flying machine has disappeared. I cannot even take a bath without having a hundred or two people peeking at me. Fortunately, everyone seems to be filled with a spirit of friendliness."*
>
> Wilbur Wright in a letter to his sister Katharine, August 1908

that had once called them *bluffeurs* apologized publicly for doubting their ability to fly. After more than a decade of working on "the flying problem," the Wright brothers were now world-famous as the inventors of the airplane.

Back in the United States

Meanwhile, in the United States, Orville was having similar success with his demonstrations. He made his first public

RACE FOR THE SKIES

During the years the Wright brothers refused to demonstrate their airplane, most aviators believed the race to fly was still on. The French, in particular, wanted to win that race.

By 1905, a number of French fliers had managed a few short flights in copies of Wright gliders. But it was a Brazilian aviator, flying in France, who made the first significant headway. In an awkward, box kite-shaped machine, Alberto Santos-Dumont flew 197 feet (60 m) in October 1906. He was hailed as the first person to fly a heavier-than-air craft in Europe. The aircraft was not capable of *controlled* flight, though, so Alberto went back to the drawing board.

By this time, designer Gabriel Voisin had also entered the flying race. In early 1907, after partnering with other aviators, he opened an aircraft factory with his brother Charles. The pair immediately built two

Brazilian aviator Alberto Santos-Dumont (top) is shown in 1906 (above) flying the first heavier-than-air craft in Europe.

French aviation pioneers Gabriel (left) and Charles Voisin.

flight in the *Model A Flyer* on September 3, 1908, at Fort Myer, Virginia—just across the Potomac River from Washington, D.C. Over the next two weeks, he performed increasingly demanding flights. Like his brother, he began drawing crowds to the military base that served as the site of his flight tests.

Orville also began breaking records Wilbur had set in France,

successful planes, beating Alberto's attempt to design an aircraft capable of controlled flight. The Voisin aircraft were considered the first successful flying machines in Europe.

Paris-born aviator Henri Farman bought one of the Voisin brothers' 1907 planes. In it, he set a number of speed and distance records. He also made significant modifications to the plane, which came to be known as the *Voisin-Farman I*. In November 1907, Henri became the first person in Europe to stay in the air for more than one minute. Two months later, he was the first to fly a complete circle.

Between 1905 and 1907 Gabriel Voisin had partnered with another French flier, Louis Blériot. Together, they built three planes, none of which flew. After they went their separate ways, Louis found success. With the launch of the *Blériot VII*, in November 1907, he joined Henri Farman as one of France's most celebrated fliers. During the first half of 1908, the two aviators constantly outdid each other with new feats of flight.

Then Wilbur Wright arrived on the scene. With his *Model A Flyer*, he dazzled French fans, demonstrating to the world that the race to fly had actually ended five years earlier, when he and Orville had flown the original *Flyer* at Kitty Hawk.

French aviators Henri Farman (left) and Gabriel Voisin were friends and rivals when they teamed up to design, produce, and fly the craft known as the Voisin-Farman I. A disagreement eventually ended Henri's partnership with Gabriel and Charles Voisin.

French aviation pioneer Louis Blériot.

staying in the air for more than an hour at a time. Day after day, Orville stayed in the air longer and longer, breaking his own endurance records.

At the army's request, Orville began taking passengers on his flights. On September 17, an army officer named Lieutenant Thomas Selfridge climbed into the cockpit beside the pilot. The flight started off smoothly enough, but a few minutes after takeoff, one of the propellers cracked, split apart, and smashed into the plane's wings and wires. The *Model A Flyer* spun out of control, plunging to the ground nose-first.

Bystanders ran to the wrecked plane. They found Orville bleeding and unconscious, and Thomas trapped in the rubble. They freed Thomas and rushed both men to a hospital.

Orville suffered a broken leg, four broken ribs, a back injury, and a dislocated hip. Thomas was in even worse shape. He died that night in surgery.

A few minutes after takeoff during a test run for the U.S. Army on September 27, 1908, a split propeller caused the Model A Flyer *to spin out of control. The crash seriously injured Orville and took the life of his passenger, Lieutenant. Thomas Selfridge.*

As soon as she heard about the crash, Orville's sister Katharine rushed to Virginia. At the time, she was working as a schoolteacher in Dayton. She left her job and remained by her brother's hospital bed for the next seven weeks.

Despite Thomas's death, army officials assured Orville that they still wanted to buy a Wright aircraft. They extended the brothers' contract to give Orville time to recover.

When Orville was well enough to travel, he and Katharine went to France to visit their elder brother, who was still setting flight records. By the time his siblings arrived in January 1909, Wilbur had set altitude, distance, and duration records. He had flown the world's first female passenger. He was treated like royalty, with celebrations, dinners, and ceremonies in his honor. When Katharine and Orville arrived in France, they were surprised to find that they were as famous as Wilbur was.

In February, the Wrights moved their flight center to the warmer climate of Pau, a town in southern France, near the border with Spain. Their fans and the media followed. The public couldn't get enough of the Wright brothers and their famous flying machine. Orville was still unable to pilot a plane because of his accident, but Wilbur gave rides to the rich and the royal, politicians and photographers. He also gave flying lessons to a few French aviators, so they could fly the *Model A Flyer* after the Wrights had moved on.

After a brief trip to Italy, where Wilbur taught members of the Italian military to fly,

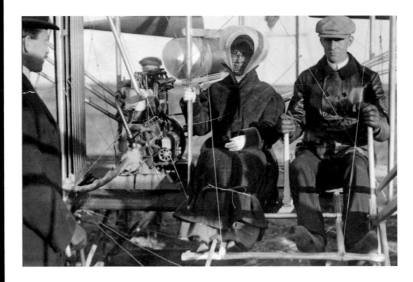

Above: On February 15, 1909, in Le Mans, France, Wilbur Wright took his sister Katharine for her first-ever airplane ride. She is shown here, with Wilbur at the controls, bundled up for protection from the wind. Wilbur and Orville (shown at left) also tied a rope around her overcoat and skirts to keep them from billowing up.

Following Katharine's flight with Wilbur, she became an instant celebrity, especially in the United States. In this newspaper piece from April 1909, not only is she shown at the controls of the Wright plane, but Wilbur is nowhere to be seen!

The American Girl Whom All Europe Is Watching

Katherine Wright, the "Silent Partner" of Orville and Wilbur Wright, Who Has Aided in the Aerial Triumphs of the Intrepid Brothers, and Who Is Soon to Return to America to Assist by Her Counsel in New and More Daring Enterprises.

the Wright brothers and
sister headed for home.
Wilbur and Orville still
had a contract to complete
with the U.S. Army—
the work that had
been interrupted by
Orville's crash.

The trio of siblings
sailed into New York
Harbor in early May
1909—and they were
shocked by the welcome
they received! Word of
their success in France
had obviously spread to
the United States. They
were greeted as national
heroes. Fans, reporters,
and photographers swarmed the Wrights
everywhere they went.

Wilbur gives an informal demonstration of the Model A Flyer's *controls to King Alfonso XIII of Spain in Pau, France, near the Spanish border.*

After a day in New York City, the brothers
and sister returned to Dayton, where
thousands of well-wishers greeted them. A
few weeks later, on June 10, 1909, President
William Taft invited the three Wrights to the
White House, where he presented each of the
brothers with the Congressional Medal of
Honor, the Samuel P. Langley Gold Medal for
Aerodromics, and a medal from the Aero Club
of America. In mid-June, the city of Dayton
held a two-day celebration in the Wright
brothers' honor. They were treated to parades,
receptions, concerts, ceremonies, and fireworks.
State, federal, and city politicians showered
them with medals, trophies, and awards.

Somewhere in this photo, taken in Dayton in May 1909, are Orville, Wilbur, and Katharine Wright. Upon their triumphant return from Europe and after a brief stop in New York City, the Wright siblings were greeted in their hometown by the thousands of friends and fans shown here.

Then, it was back to work. Two days after the fuss died down, the brothers traveled to Fort Myer to continue where Orville had left off nine months earlier.

Soaring to New Heights

On June 29, for the first time since his terrible accident, Orville sat in the pilot's seat of a *Model A Flyer*, and took to the sky. A month later, he flew a number of demonstrations to prove the plane could travel at the speed, distance, and altitude the U.S. Army had demanded. With that, at the end of July the army

Wilbur (left) and Orville accept awards at the Wright Brothers Homecoming Celebration in Dayton on July 18, 1909.

finally signed on the dotted line and bought its first aircraft from the Wright brothers. The price tag was $30,000— the equivalent of about $750,000 in today's dollars.

After the brothers' success in demonstrating and selling planes in the United States and France, buyers in other countries were determined to become part of this new aircraft industry.

In the fall of 1909, Orville and Katharine traveled to Germany to meet with a group of investors who had formed a company to manufacture Wright planes there. In Berlin, Orville dazzled thousands of German fans the same way his brother had impressed the French a year earlier. He also set new altitude and flight duration records while he was there.

While his brother was astonishing Europeans, Wilbur continued to wow Americans. In September, as part of New York City's Hudson-Fulton Celebration, he flew over New York Harbor, then circled the Statue of Liberty. Hundreds of vessels had sailed into the harbor for the occasion. Their crews, along with thousands of shore-bound New Yorkers, witnessed the historic flight.

The *New York Evening Sun* reported on Wilbur's feat: "The harbor craft shrieked their welcomes, and the cheering men and women

Lieutenant Frank Lahm (seated, left), sits with Orville Wright (seated at right) as they prepare to test fly a Wright plane in July 1909. With that flight, the craft was named Signal Corps No. 1. It became the U.S. Army's first aircraft. Lieutenant Lahm became the first certified military pilot.

FLYING INTO THE SPOTLIGHT

In July 1909, as Wilbur and Orville Wright prepared to demonstrate their aircraft to the U.S. military, another aviator made history—and temporarily stole the brothers' spotlight.

On July 25, French pilot Louis Blériot became the first person to fly across the English Channel.

The quest to conquer the body of water separating France and England had begun nine months earlier. In October 1908, a British publisher announced he would pay £1,000 ($4,900) to the first pilot to cross the channel by air. The publisher—and most of the aviation world—assumed Wilbur would be the one to make the historic flight. Wilbur didn't want to risk crashing, though, so he declined to compete for the prize.

The following July, three French pilots parked their planes near Calais, France, ready to take the English Channel challenge. The first pilot landed his plane in the water. The second crashed during a test flight. That left Blériot to give it a try.

At about 4:40 on the morning of July 25, Louis took off from Calais. He crash-landed in Dover, England, 36 and a half minutes later.

With that, Louis Blériot became an international hero. His flight was neither the longest distance nor longest duration ever flown, but it was the world's first long-distance flight over open water.

French aviator Louis Blériot made history, and headlines, in 1909 when he became the first pilot to fly a heavier-than-air craft across the English Channel. This poster shows Louis approaching the coast of Dover, England, toward the end of his journey. Two men are waving flags to signal him—one the flag of France, the other a flag used on British commercial ships.

ashore bore witness that our Lady of Liberty had been visited by one of her children in a vessel needing only the winds on which to sail."

A week later, Wilbur made another flight in New York airspace as part of the Hudson-Fulton Celebration. This time, he flew up and down the Hudson River, with an estimated one million people watching from the ground and from the windows of Manhattan skyscrapers. This was the first time most of them had ever seen an airplane!

By the time Orville and Katharine returned from Germany in November, they—along with Wilbur—were among the most famous people in the country. The trio spent the rest of the year attending ceremonies, dinners, and parties in their honor.

Wilbur Wright (back to camera) examines a canoe attachment on the Wright Model A Flyer *as he prepares for his first flight over water as part of the 1909 Hudson-Fulton Celebration in New York City.*

Spectators along the Hudson River in New York City watch Wilbur flying the Model A Flyer *during the 1909 Hudson-Fulton Celebration.*

At the same time, a group of wealthy American businessmen offered to finance the brothers' airplane business. The Wright Company was incorporated in November 1909, with Wilbur as president and Orville as a vice-president.

After years of struggle, it appeared the sky was the limit for the Wright brothers. As it turned out, though, another American aviator was about to bring them down to Earth.

Orville, Katharine, and Wilbur Wright in 1909.

THE WRIGHT SISTER

Katharine was the youngest, and only girl, of the Wright siblings. When the kids' mom died, 14-year-old Katharine became the lady of the house, looking after her brothers and their father, Milton.

When Kate, as she was called, was 19, Milton sent her to Oberlin College in northern Ohio. There, she earned a teaching degree. She was the only Wright sibling to finish college.

After graduation, Kate moved back to Dayton to live with Orville, Wilbur, and Milton. She got a job teaching at the local high school. In 1908, when Orville was seriously injured in a plane crash, Kate left her job to nurse him back to health.

Over the years, Kate served as her brothers' unofficial business manager. After Wilbur and Orville found success with their aircraft, Kate's role as business and social manager became official. At this point, she was so much a part of the family aircraft work that it became a Wright brothers-and-sister business. Kate was included in every ceremony and celebration in the brothers' honor.

Because of her dedication to her family, Kate remained single until she was in her 50s. In 1925, she reconnected with a college sweetheart, newspaper owner and editor Henry J. Haskell. She married him in 1926 and moved to Kansas City, Missouri.

When their mother died in 1889, Orville and Katharine were teenagers, and in

a sense Kate became the "woman of the house." As they grew older, Orville came to depend on her more. He took her marriage as a kind of rejection of him as a brother. For almost three years, he refused to see her—until he heard she was dying. Early in 1929, Katharine contracted pneumonia. Orville was at her side when she died on March 3, 1929, at age 54.

Kate's husband built a fountain in her honor at Oberlin College, and the National Aeronautic Association awards an annual Katharine Wright Trophy to an individual who has supported or made a personal contribution to the advancement of aviation.

In this detail from a photo of a family gathering at the home of Orville in Dayton, Katharine Wright is shown with Orville and their father Milton, seated next to Katharine.

Chapter 5
The Ups and Downs of Living Wright

By 1909, Wilbur and Orville Wright were considered two of the world's most famous fliers—but they certainly weren't the only ones taking to the skies. At the same time, several French and U.S. aviators were testing flying machines of their own. One fellow in particular, an American motorcycle manufacturer named Glenn Curtiss, was nipping at the Wright brothers' heels—and causing them all kinds of legal headaches.

Patent Wars

Back in 1906, the U.S. Patent Office had approved the Wrights' patent for a "Flying Machine." Legally, that meant nobody

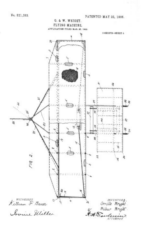

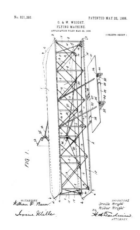

Two of the many diagrams that Orville and Wilbur Wright provided on their application for a patent in 1903. These pages appear as they did on the approved patent, issued by the U.S. Patent Office in 1906, for the brothers' "Flying Machine." For years to come, the principles in this patent became the object of disputes between aviation companies on both sides of the Atlantic. The Wright brothers were at the center of most of the disagreements.

PATENT PROTECTION

A patent is a legal agreement that protects an inventor from someone else stealing his or her discovery. It means nobody else can manufacture, use, or sell the invention for a given period of time. Today, in the United States and Canada, this period is 20 years. The government grants patents in exchange for a full description of the invention, which might be a machine, a process for making something, or a change to a previously patented product.

To get a patent, the invention has to be new and useful, and not so obvious that just anyone with the same skill set as the inventor could have come up with it. It also has to be tangible, meaning it is a thing you can touch, or a process designed to create something you can touch.

Back in the Wright brothers' day, aerodynamic principles were new, incredibly complicated concepts for non-scientists to get their brains around. That meant different judges in different countries had their own ideas about whether the principles should be covered by the Wright brothers' patent. In France, for example, the judge ruled yes. In Germany, on the other hand, it was a no.

could use the brothers' ideas without their permission.

The key concept protected by the patent was a three-part system that allowed a pilot to control an aircraft in flight. The three mechanisms worked together—the elevator to control pitch, the tail rudder to control yaw, and the moveable wingtips to control roll.

Mastering these three aerodynamic principles—pitch, yaw, and roll—continues to be the secret to controlled flight today.

Because they had discovered these principles, Wilbur and Orville believed they owned the rights to any aircraft design that incorporated them—and anyone who used the principles should have to pay for the privilege.

Because no aircraft can fly without some sort of three-dimensional control system, that would mean every designer and every builder of every aircraft ever invented would owe the Wrights money.

Of course, the brothers' competitors disagreed with this view. In the spring of 1908, after almost three years of absolute secrecy, the Wrights began demonstrating their aircraft to potential buyers. That meant their patented ideas were revealed to the world for the first time—and other aviators took note.

Wilbur and Orville may have discovered the secrets to flight, but now that their ideas were in the public eye, inventors around the world began experimenting with the aerodynamic principles the brothers had identified.

One aviator in particular challenged the Wrights' ownership of the concepts. That was Glenn Curtiss, and he became the brothers' lifelong enemy in the process.

Glenn was a member of the Aerial Experiment Association (AEA), a group of aircraft designers that included telephone inventor Alexander Graham Bell. In the summer of 1908, Glenn tested a plane he had designed. It was called the *June Bug*, and it had moveable wing flaps called ailerons.

The ailerons had been invented earlier by Bell. Members of the AEA thought the ailerons were different enough from the Wrights' system of "wing-warping" that they wouldn't violate patent rules.

The Wright brothers saw it differently. When they heard about the *June Bug*—and its ailerons—they were furious. They believed

American aviator Glenn Curtiss was a pioneer in the business of designing and building aircraft. The Wrights had flown more often, and farther, than other aviators of the day, but most of the Wrights' flights were test runs and flown in private. Glenn was much more of a self-promoter, and his flights were public events that drew huge crowds.

ARCHRIVAL

Glenn Curtiss photographed in 1909.

Glenn Curtiss was born in Hammondsport, New York, in 1878. Like the Wrights, he was in the bicycle business before he moved into aviation. Glenn started as a bicycle courier and racer, later owning his own bike shop.

Glenn loved speed so much that, in 1902, he began manufacturing motorcycles. A year later, he set a land speed record, riding 64 miles (103 km) per hour. In 1907, he rode more than double that speed, earning the title "fastest man in the world."

Glenn entered the aircraft industry in 1904. Three years later, telephone inventor Alexander Graham Bell invited him to join the Aerial Experiment Association. In 1909, Glenn launched his own aircraft company and entered a decade-long legal battle with the Wright brothers.

Glenn was a superior businessman and had a better understanding of marketing and public relations than did Wilbur and Orville. He entered aerial competitions, set flight records, and became a media darling. Because of that, his aircraft sales soared, while the Wrights' sales stalled.

In the years leading up to World War I, Glenn helped develop military aircraft technologies. He invented flying boats that could take off and land on water. He also supplied engines and aircraft to the U.S. Army during the war.

Glenn retired in 1920 and moved, with his wife and two children, to Florida. Ten years later, he died suddenly—after appendix surgery—during a business trip to New York State. He was 52 years old.

Glenn Curtiss on his V8 motorcycle in 1908, the year he set an unofficial world land speed record of over 136 miles (220 km) per hour.

Aviator and manufacturer Glenn Curtiss is shown at the controls of the June Bug *(top), a plane he designed and flew. On July 4, 1908, Glenn flew the craft for the Aero Club of America in a competition in Hammondsport, New York (bottom). For years, the Wright brothers had flown their planes out of the public eye, and Glenn's was the first officially witnessed flight in North America. It earned him a trophy, a cash award of $25,000, and a wealth of public recognition. Ironically, the Aero Club had originally offered the Wright brothers the chance to fly the plane. The Wrights were busy perfecting their* Model A Flyer *for sales to the U.S. government and buyers in France, and so they declined the offer.*

that, because the plane included one of the aerodynamic principles they had discovered, it infringed on their patent.

Because Glenn had been identified as the *June Bug*'s designer, the brothers insisted he pay for the right to use their concepts. Glenn ignored them and, in the spring of 1909, started his own aircraft manufacturing company. Four months later, he sold his first plane to the Aeronautic Society of New York.

This was the last straw for Orville and Wilbur Wright. In August 1909, they filed a lawsuit against Glenn for patent infringement.

They also asked that he be barred from building, displaying, or selling airplanes until the lawsuit was settled. At the same time, the brothers filed suit against the Aeronautic Society of New York to prevent the organization from displaying the plane it had purchased from Glenn.

The Aeronautic Society agreed to pay exhibition fees to the Wrights, but the lawsuit against Glenn Curtiss dragged on for the next eight years. In 1910, a judge ruled that Glenn was to stop building and flying airplanes. Glenn filed an appeal and continued with his aircraft business. A second judge sided with the Wrights in 1913. Again, Glenn appealed. A year later, a panel of judges once again found in favor of the Wrights and ordered Glenn to stop building airplanes. Again, Glenn resisted, and the legal mess continued.

Meanwhile, a year after Wilbur and Orville had first sued Glenn Curtiss, they also launched patent infringement lawsuits against other American, English, French, and German companies. In addition, they sued European aviators who flew Wright planes at exhibitions in the United States. Before long, aviation companies on both sides of the Atlantic were suing each other, with the Wright brothers at the center of it all.

All the legal muddling finally came to a halt in 1917. That year, the Wrights' French patent expired, and a fed-up U.S. government ordered all American aviation companies to create a patent pool. Each company was to pay a one-time fee for the right to use any aviation patent. The bulk of the pooled fees went to the

THE COMPETITION

In September 1907, Alexander Graham Bell joined with four other inventors—Canadians John McCurdy and Casey Baldwin, and Americans Glenn Curtiss and U.S. Army Lieutenant Thomas Selfridge—to form the Aerial Experiment Association (AEA). The goal of the organization, based in Nova Scotia, Canada, was to work collectively to advance aircraft development.

Canadian aviation pioneer Frederick Walker "Casey" Baldwin, shown here in 1900 as a student in St. Catharines, Ontario.

In the following months, the AEA developed four different airplanes.

Selfridge designed the first, the *Red Wing*. In it, in March 1908, Baldwin flew 319 feet (97 m), before crash-landing on a frozen lake in New York State.

Two months later, Curtiss flew 1,017 feet (310 m) in the *White Wing*, a plane designed by Baldwin. This was the first aircraft to use ailerons, developed by Bell.

In June 1908, Curtiss flew 3,000 feet (917 m) in the *June Bug*, a craft he had also designed. A few weeks later, Curtiss again took to the skies in this plane, flying 5,360 feet (1,634 m) in one minute and 40 seconds. With that, he won an aviation prize for being the first individual to fly 1 kilometer (0.6 mile) in a straight line—even though the Wright brothers had already achieved this (without winning a prize) in 1904.

The final plane built by members of the AEA was the *Silver Dart*, designed and flown by McCurdy. The craft's short flight in Nova Scotia in February 1909 was the first powered flight in Canada.

The AEA disbanded on March 31, 1909, after Curtiss secretly formed an airplane manufacturing company with another inventor.

Although not a fully trained pilot, U.S. Army Lieutenant Thomas Selfridge was the first U.S. military officer to pilot a solo flight. He also became the first person to die in the crash of a powered airplane when the Wright plane in which he was a passenger crashed in September 1908.

Wrights and to Glenn Curtiss, who by then held a number of patents of his own. With that, the rivals agreed to put the patent issues to rest, once and for all.

By this time, the rest of the European lawsuits had already been settled—some for, some against, the Wright brothers.

The Price of the Patents

Whether Orville and Wilbur were right to file lawsuits against their competitors is something aviation historians continue to debate. One thing everyone agrees on, though, is that the brothers paid a huge personal price for their legal actions.

As the patent wars raged around them, the Wright brothers' public image suffered. Once considered American heroes, Wilbur and Orville were now viewed by many people as greedy, unfair, and unpleasant. Opponents blamed them for blocking the future of American aviation innovation.

There's certainly no question that the brothers' legal activities hampered their *own* aviation innovation.

In November 1909, with the help of wealthy investors, the brothers had launched the Wright Company to build airplanes. Within a year, their manufacturing facility in Dayton, Ohio, was producing two planes a month.

By this time, though, the patent wars were in full swing. That meant the brothers now had two full-time jobs—running the airplane company and managing the legal mess.

They decided that Orville would be in charge of the booming manufacturing side

The Wright Company factory, photographed in 1911.

of the company, and Wilbur would focus on the lawsuits.

The problem with this arrangement was that Wilbur was the idea-man of the duo. Orville was good at fine-tuning his brother's designs and putting them into practice. Without Wilbur's full-time presence, though, the Wright Company began to lag behind when it came to advances in aviation technology.

Still, the brothers managed a few innovations during the next two years. Early in 1910, they established the United State's first flying school and test flight center. That summer, they launched the Wright Fliers aerial exhibition team. The team was disbanded in November 1911 after two pilots died during air shows.

In the fall of 1910, the Wrights unveiled two new planes at an international air show at Belmont Park, a horse-racing facility on Long Island, just outside of New York City. The *Wright Model B*, an updated version of the successful *Model A*, had added features, including wheels and a tail elevator. (The *Model A* had had a forward elevator.) The second new craft, a racing plane called the *Wright Model R*, flew an astounding 70 miles (113 km) per hour at the same air show. Unfortunately, it crashed before it could enter any races.

At the end of 1910, a *Wright Model B* made the world's first air cargo shipment. A few months later, the same type of plane was used in the world's first military scouting mission. At the end of 1911, a specially designed Wright aircraft became the first in the world to cross a continent. Pilot Cal Rodgers flew from New York to California in 84 days.

In October of 1911, Orville Wright returned to Kitty Hawk. There, he tested a new glider and set a record for soaring—nine minutes, 45 seconds. It would be ten years before this time was beaten.

Other than these few developments, the Wright Company was more or less stalled when it came to developing new and better airplanes. Sales slowed and—even worse—Wright aircraft were no longer considered the best in the sky.

By this time, other aviators, including Glenn Curtiss, had built faster, less expensive, easier-to-operate planes.

Orville (left) and Wilbur Wright at the Belmont Park International Aviation Tournament on Long Island, New York, in 1910.

The Wright Model R, *built for speed and altitude competitions, was also called the "Baby Grand." It is shown here at Belmont Park in 1910.*

CALBRAITH ROGERS

1ST. AVIATOR TO CROSS THE CONTINENT

HIS FATAL WRECK — LONG BEACH — CAL.

Left: Cal Rogers is shown on this postcard at the controls during his historic transcontinental flight in 1911. Right: In 1912, while performing an exhibition flight over Long Beach, California, his plane ran into a flock of birds, causing the plane to crash. Cal died from his injuries.

In 1911, Orville returned to Kitty Hawk to fly a new glider based on a 1911 machine, but without the motor. In this photo, he is shown testing the craft for safety and stability against the strong winds at Kitty Hawk.

THE WRIGHT STUFF

On May 25, 1910, Orville and Wilbur Wright flew together for the first, and only, time. Years earlier, their father had forbidden the two to fly together. He feared a plane crash would take his two youngest sons from him. The brothers, too, realized it would not be in their best interests to take to the skies together. If the plane crashed, and both of them died, who would carry on with their work? The same day the brothers flew together, Orville took his father for his first-ever flight. On that day, 82-year-old Milton became the oldest person to fly anywhere in the world. During the six-minute flight, the crowd below heard Milton yelling, "Higher, Orville, higher!"

Research, development, and experimentation were Wilbur's strengths—and he just wasn't around to do any of it anymore.

Throughout 1911, Wilbur spent most of his energy tackling business and legal matters. He was consumed by mounds of paperwork, endless meetings, lengthy court appearances, and exhausting travel schedules. He spent months on end in Europe working with lawyers, investors, and business partners. When he returned to the United States, Wilbur was constantly on the move, traveling between Dayton, New York, and Fort Myer.

By early May 1912, Wilbur was so drained, physically and emotionally, that he contracted typhoid fever. A few weeks later, on May 30, he died in his childhood bedroom in the family home in Dayton, Ohio. He was just 45 years old.

THE WRIGHT STUFF

The last time Wilbur Wright ever flew one of his beloved airplanes was in Germany, in June 1911—a full year before he died.

> *"We wished to be free from business cares so that we could give all our own time to advancing the science and art of aviation, but we have been compelled to spend our time on business matters instead, during the past five years. When we think what we might have accomplished if we had been able to devote this time to experiments, we feel very sad, but it is always easier to deal with things than with men, and no one can direct his life entirely as he would choose."*

Wilbur Wright, in a letter to a friend, January 25, 1912

The unmistakable profile of Wilbur Wright as he pilots one of the Wright brothers' early gliders.

Chapter 6
Flying Solo

When Wilbur Wright died, the whole world mourned. International newspapers reported on the passing of "the man who made flying possible." World leaders sent their condolences. The Wright family received masses of flowers and thousands of telegrams of sympathy from around the globe. Twenty-five thousand people paid their respects at a public viewing of Wilbur's coffin. "Wilbur is dead and buried!" wrote his father Milton after a private funeral. "We are all stricken. It does not seem possible he is gone. Probably Orville and Katharine felt his loss most. They say little."

Orville Alone

Upon Wilbur's death, Orville became president of the Wright Company. In addition, he and Katharine picked up the patent fights where

Led by Orville Wright (walking toward camera), pallbearers carry Wilbur Wright's casket out of the First Presbyterian Church in Dayton following Wilbur's funeral service in 1912.

Upon Wilbur's death, Orville and Katharine stayed close both personally and professionally. In this photo, Katharine, wearing a leather jacket, cap, and goggles, is shown with Orville aboard a Wright Model HS *airplane in 1915.*

their older brother had left off. They believed the lengthy legal struggle had led to Wilbur's early death.

Over the next few years, the Wright Company was plagued by a series of airplane crashes. Between 1912 and 1914, at least ten people died in Wright aircraft. This led the government (and others) to question the safety, stability, and design of Wright planes—especially the *Model C.*

Launched in 1912, the *Wright Model C* was a more powerful version of the popular *Model B.* Six *Model C*s owned by the army crashed, killing their occupants.

The government blamed the aircraft. Orville blamed the pilots. To prevent further crashes, he invented an early version of autopilot to ensure the *Model C* could not stall and nose-dive. The device earned a prestigious aviation award, but soon became outdated when another inventor created a better system. The *Wright Model C* was grounded for good in February 1914.

By then, Wright aircraft had lost favor in the flying community in general. While the Wrights had been consumed by patent battles, aviation technology had continued without them.

Compared to new models by other designers, Wright aircraft were now seen as clunky, complicated, unsafe, and out of date. At this point, Orville found himself in a predicament. If he didn't update his aircraft, his already slow sales would fall even faster. On the other hand, updating his designs meant incorporating some of the technological advances of his competitors—the people he and Wilbur had accused of stealing their ideas.

Orville was now in his early 40s, and his heart wasn't in the business side of flying. He had never liked being a manager, and he hated meetings.

His lack of interest, coupled with the slowing market and thriving competition—not to mention the series of crashes—led Orville to a surprising decision.

In 1915, he sold his shares in the Wright Company—along with the patents he and Wilbur had fought so hard to protect—to a group of New York City-based investors. A year later, the Wright Company merged with another aircraft manufacturer to become the Wright-Martin Company. In 1919, it was renamed the Wright Aeronautical Company. Ironically, in 1929, Wright Aeronautical merged with a company founded by the brothers' enemy Glenn Curtiss. The Curtiss-Wright Corporation remains in business today.

THE WRIGHT STUFF

In the summer of 1916, Orville treated his father and sister to an extended vacation in Ontario, Canada. They liked it so much that Orville bought Lambert Island, a tiny, crescent-shaped island in Georgian Bay (shown here at sunset). Orville and various relatives spent summers there for the next 20 years.

In 1917, Orville also allowed the Wright name to be used by another aircraft firm, the Dayton-Wright Company. The company was formed at the time war was declared between the United States and Germany during World War I. Orville served as an occasional consultant for this organization, but otherwise, had little to do with it. In 1923, the Dayton-Wright Company was closed by its parent company, General Motors, which had bought it in 1919.

The Dayton-Wright OW.1 Aerial Coupe *was a pioneering aircraft: a four-seat, single-engine civilian passenger plane with an enclosed cabin. It was the last aircraft designed by Orville Wright, which is why its name includes the initials "OW."*

Another Wright Fight

In 1916, after retiring from the Wright Company, Orville built himself a private office and workshop in downtown Dayton. He called it the Wright Aeronautical Laboratory. There, he continued to develop aircraft ideas and other inventions. He worked to improve airplane engines, landing gear, and wing mechanics. He built household appliances for Hawthorn Hill, the family's new mansion, and toys for his nieces and nephews. He also used the space to rebuild the original 1903 *Wright Flyer*.

By this time, Orville was embroiled in yet another battle—one that called into question the Wright brothers' claim that they invented the airplane. Again, the Wrights' archrival, Glenn Curtiss, was at the heart of the conflict.

It all stemmed from events that had taken place 13 years earlier. On December 17, 1903,

In the spring of 1914, Orville—along with his father Milton and sister Kate—moved out of the Hawthorn Street home in Dayton, Ohio, where they'd lived for 42 years. They moved to this mansion, designed by Orville, on the outskirts of Dayton. Wilbur was also meant to live in the house, but he died in 1912, before it was completed. Orville lived at the house they called Hawthorn Hill for the rest of his life.

the Wright brothers had made their famous first flight at Kitty Hawk. Nine days earlier, though, another pilot had flight-tested the *"Great Aerodrome,"* a craft designed by Samuel Pierpont Langley.

Based on Langley's unmanned 1896 *Aerodrome*, the 1903 version was bigger, faster, and more powerful—and it crashed spectacularly into the Potomac River as soon as it took off. The *Aerodrome* never flew, and its inventor died in 1906.

That was the end of the *Aerodrome* until 1914, when Glenn Curtiss lost his lawsuit to the Wright brothers.

At that point, Glenn offered to rebuild the *Aerodrome* for its owner, the Smithsonian Institution. He said he wanted to study the aircraft's design. What he *really* wanted to do was use the *Aerodrome* to prove that Orville and Wilbur Wright had *not* been the first to build an airplane capable of flight.

Instead of merely rebuilding the 1903 *Aerodrome*, Glenn made significant modifications to it. With those changes, the craft became flight-worthy. Glenn made a few short flights in it.

He and the Smithsonian then argued that the *Aerodrome* had, in fact, been the world's first flyable plane—even though it hadn't gotten off the ground until *after* Glenn's adaptations.

Immediately after proving the *Aerodrome* could fly, Glenn returned it to its original state, undoing the changes he'd made to it. The Smithsonian exhibited the original, unflyable, *Great Aerodrome* for the next 28 years, calling it the world's first flyable aircraft.

A pilot working for manufacturer Glenn Curtiss attempts to get a craft called the Aerodrome *to rise above the surface of a lake in 1914. The craft had failed previous tests in 1903. Glenn, a rival of the Wrights, refurbished it in 1914. He did so in an effort to prove that it, and not the Wrights'* Flyer, *was the first to achieve controlled flight.*

Of course, Orville was outraged over the Smithsonian's claim. He set out to restore his, and Wilbur's, reputation as the inventors of the airplane. In 1916, he rebuilt the original 1903 *Wright Flyer* to help him prove that he and his brother had been the first to fly.

After displaying it at a number of venues, Orville stored the *Flyer* at his workshop—until he'd had enough of the Smithsonian's foolishness.

For years, he'd tried reasoning with the institution, offering documented proof and scientific evidence. Eventually, Orville realized the only way he would convince Smithsonian leaders to admit they'd misrepresented the *Aerodrome* was to shame them into doing so.

In 1926, he announced his intention to ship the *Flyer* to the Science Museum in London,

Orville with Scipio, a St. Bernard he acquired in 1917.

WERE THE WRIGHT BROTHERS *REALLY FIRST?*

There are people today who believe the Wright brothers did not invent the airplane. Some say it was New Zealand inventor Richard Pearse in 1902 (or 1903, depending on who you ask). In a 1909 newspaper article, Richard said he had "conceived the idea of inventing a flying machine" when he was young, but "I did not attempt anything practical with the idea until 1904."

New Zealand aviation pioneer Richard Pearse.

Gustave Whitehead and a single-winged craft, possibly in 1901.

Other Wright doubters say a German-American named Gustave Whitehead (born Gustav Weisskopf) was the first to fly. Five people are reported to have witnessed his first flight in August 1901, in Connecticut—but the story of Gustave's flight did not surface until 1937. Tom Crouch, a curator at the National Air and Space Museum, says it's not true. What is true, said Tom, is that Whitehead built a number of flying machines after the Wright brothers' 1903 flights, but "not one of those powered machines ever left the ground. Either Whitehead had somehow forgotten the secrets of flight, or he had never flown a powered machine at all."

Similarly, some people question the Wright brothers' claim to have flown in 1903. The famous photograph of the event proved the *Flyer* was not flight-worthy, they say, and the five people who said they witnessed the Kitty Hawk flights weren't experts.

On the other hand, a panel of aviation experts watched Brazilian aviator Alberto Santos-Dumont fly in Paris in 1906. And because Alberto's flight was witnessed by experts, the flight was certified as "first."

At least five other inventors from around the globe have been put forward as the first humans to fly a powered aircraft. Most have been discounted—but the discussion continues!

A cartoon caricature of Brazilian aviation pioneer Alberto Santos-Dumont in a 1901 issue of Vanity Fair *magazine.*

England. The news created a public outcry—an American national treasure was about to be shipped overseas! Said Orville:

"I believe that my course in sending our Kitty Hawk machine to a foreign museum is the only way of correcting the history of the flying-machine, which by false and misleading statements, has been perverted by the Smithsonian Institution."

Still, the Smithsonian didn't back down.

In 1928, the *Flyer* arrived in London, where it remained until 1942. That year, the Smithsonian finally caved in to public pressure and admitted the *Wright Flyer* had, in fact, been the world's first flying machine.

By this time, though, World War II was in full swing. To ensure the historic aircraft survived the conflict, it was placed in a bombproof storage chamber in England until the war was over.

It took another few years to work out shipping details, but finally, in the fall of 1948,

The 1903 Wright Flyer, with a mannequin of Wilbur Wright at the controls, on exhibit at the National Air and Space Museum of the Smithsonian Institution in Washington, D.C.

"*Death came to Orville Wright last night, 44 years after he put wings on the world with the first flight in a heavier-than-air machine. The 76-year-old co-inventor of the airplane died in his sleep.*"

Associated Press,
January 31, 1948

the *Wright Flyer* returned to the United States. To great fanfare, the flying machine took its rightful place at the Smithsonian Institution, identified as "the world's first power-driven heavier-than-air machine, in which man made free, controlled, and sustained flight."

Sadly, Orville Wright did not live to see this day. On January 27, 1948, he suffered his second heart attack in four months. The 76-year-old died in a Dayton hospital three days later, on January 30. Orville was buried in the family plot, alongside his mother Susan, brother Wilbur, father Milton (who died in 1917), and sister Kate (who died in 1929).

THE WRIGHT STUFF

Orville Wright piloted a plane, a *Wright Model B*, for the last time in 1918. He had intended to continue flying for the rest of his life. He had to give it up, though, because of pain and stiffness he still suffered from after the Fort Myer crash a decade earlier.

Wright Twilight

Orville's passing marked the end of an era in the aviation industry. No longer was the world learning to fly—Orville and Wilbur had taken care of that. By this time, cloth and wood flying machines had given way to jets, rockets, and planes that flew so fast that they broke the sound barrier.

During the final decades of his life, Orville continued to participate in the evolution of flight. He served as an aviation adviser and board member with various organizations. In 1920, President Woodrow Wilson appointed him to the board of the new National Advisory Committee for Aeronautics (now NASA, the National Aeronautics and Space Administration). In 1926, Orville joined

CHARLES LINDBERGH AT YOUR SERVICE

In May 1927, in a plane called *Spirit of St. Louis*, American pilot Charles Lindbergh made history when he became the first person to fly solo across the Atlantic Ocean. His flight from New York City to Paris took 33 hours, 30 minutes, making him an instant international hero.

Upon his return to the United States after his famous flight, Charles stopped in Dayton, Ohio, to pay tribute to Orville Wright. After that, the two aviators stayed in touch, crossing paths on occasion, for years to come.

In 1934, with the Smithsonian Institution refusing to acknowledge the Wright brothers' *Flyer* as the first aircraft capable of controlled flight, Charles wrote to Orville. He offered his help in "arranging to bring the original Kitty Hawk airplane back to the United States to be placed permanently in the National Museum in Washington."

Orville Wright (left) and Charles Lindbergh (right) are shown with a military official at Wilbur Wright Field, near Dayton, on June 22, 1927. The visit took place shortly after Lindbergh's historic flight across the Atlantic.

Charles met with Orville and Smithsonian representatives, but was unable to resolve the conflict. His conclusion? "The fault lies primarily with the Smithsonian … [Orville] has encountered the narrow mindedness of science and dishonesty of commerce."

Years later, Charles again showed his respect for his elder aviation colleagues. For 20 years, his *Spirit of St. Louis* had been the centerpiece of the institution's Arts and Industries Building. In 1948, when the *Wright Flyer* finally took its rightful place at the Smithsonian, Charles graciously agreed that his famous plane should be moved from the position of honor to make room for it.

Orville Wright in 1928, at around 57 years of age. During the last few decades of his life, he continued to contribute to the advancement of flight and the aviation industry.

the board of the Guggenheim Fund for the Promotion of Aeronautics, an organization that funds and promotes education and research in the field. In 1936, he was elected to the National Academy of Sciences.

Over the years, Orville's contributions to flight were celebrated with awards, special medals, and 11 honorary university degrees. (Neither Wright brother graduated from college, but they had 15 honorary degrees between them.)

Orville took his final flight as a passenger in 1944. His last major aviation-related project was to oversee restoration of the original 1905 *Wright Flyer III*. It is now on display at Carillon Historical Park in Dayton.

Today, a number of major memorials mark the locations where the Wright brothers flew. The largest is the Wright Brothers National Memorial, near Kitty Hawk, where Orville and Wilbur made their historic first flights.

In the city of Dayton, Ohio, where the Wrights lived and worked most of their lives, there are more than a dozen sculptures, landmarks, and memorials. In 1937, the Wrights' original Dayton home and bicycle shop were relocated to Greenfield Village at the Henry Ford Museum in Dearborn, Michigan.

The 1903 *Wright Flyer* remains on display at the Smithsonian Institution in Washington, D.C. It was featured in the popular movie *Night at the Museum: Battle of the Smithsonian* in 2009. The film's writers, Robert Ben Garant and Thomas Lennon, played Orville and Wilbur in the film.

The Wright Cycle Company in 1937 after being moved to the Henry Ford Museum in Dearborn, Michigan. Behind the shop, the Wrights constructed an addition where they built their first plane.

In 2000, the Smithsonian also verified the discovery of a new species of moth, which was then named *Glyphidocera wrightorum*, after the brothers. The moth was discovered at Huffman Prairie, the pastureland outside of Dayton where, starting in 1904, the Wrights had performed some of the most important testing for their aircraft. In 1917, the U.S. Army leased land on and near Huffman Prairie to use for its own aviation work, naming the area Wilbur Wright Field. Over the next few years, other lands were added to this tract, and the name Wilbur Wright Field gave way to simply Wright Field. Finally, in 1948, the newly formed U.S. Air Force merged Wright Field with nearby Patterson Field to create Wright-Patterson Air Force Base, which remains in use today as a major U.S. military installation.

Museums around the globe continue to showcase the work of these introverted inventors, and dozens of authors and filmmakers have documented their story.

"We dared to hope we had invented something that would bring lasting peace to the Earth. But we were wrong. We underestimated man's capacity to hate and to corrupt good means for an evil end. No, I don't have any regrets about my part in the invention of the airplane, though no one could deplore more than I the destruction it has caused."

Orville Wright, 1943

ANOTHER WRIGHT RIVALRY

Two U.S. states claim Orville and Wilbur Wright as their own when it comes to taking credit for the brothers' aviation successes. In Ohio, vehicle license plates read "Birthplace of Aviation." In North Carolina, the slogan on the state's license plates is "First in Flight." How can both be true?

Both are, in fact, correct in their claims.

Orville and Wilbur lived most of their lives in Dayton, Ohio. There, they toiled in their workshop on flight-related ideas and experiments. The *idea* of aviation was born in the Wrights' minds in Ohio. The components of the first plane were also built there.

On the other hand, the Wrights' first *flights* took place at Kitty Hawk, North Carolina, making that state's claim true, too.

Both states played major roles in the brothers' early years, and both are right to celebrate the Wrights' important aviation contributions.

In 2003, the United States Mint issued a special 2003 First Flight Centennial Silver Dollar to honor the Wright brothers' history-making flights at Kitty Hawk.

Today, Wilbur and Orville Wright are celebrated the world over as the fathers of flight, the men who taught the world to fly, the brothers who soared skyward.

Thanks to their imaginations, their observations, and their dreams, we now have jet planes, rockets, and the International Space Station. Even modern drones use the principals of flight identified by Wilbur and Orville more than a century ago.

When the Wright brothers first played with their little flying toy, their beloved "bat," most people didn't believe human flight was even possible. These curious kids believed otherwise. They experimented. They read. They pondered. They endured failure and ridicule—but they refused to give up. In the end, the Wright brothers did the impossible. They gave us the sky.

Shown here is a detail from a long band, called the Frieze of American History, *that encircles the dome of the U.S. Capitol in Washington, D.C. Called "The Birth of Aviation," this section shows Orville Wright in the* Flyer *and Wilbur running alongside to steady it. Behind them are aviation pioneers Leonardo da Vinci, Samuel Pierpont Langley, and Octave Chanute, each holding a model of his earlier design for a flying machine.*

Chronology

April 16, 1867 Wilbur Wright is born in Millville, Indiana.

August 19, 1871 Orville Wright is born in Dayton, Ohio.

1878 Milton Wright gives sons Wilbur and Orville a flying toy they call "the bat."

1884 After moving many times, Wright family settles permanently in Dayton.

1886 Wilbur struck in face by a hockey stick, knocking out his teeth and ending his plans to go to Yale University.

1889 Orville quits high school to open print shop; Wilbur joins business; mother Susan dies of tuberculosis.

1892 Brothers open bicycle repair shop.

1896–1899 Read all they can find about flight; Wilbur writes to Smithsonian Institution, requesting all information it has on subject; brothers realize key to aircraft lies in ability to control it.

1900 Make first trip to Kitty Hawk, North Carolina, to test their first glider; after several flights, glider destroyed in wind.

1901 **Summer:** test another glider at Kitty Hawk; it is a complete failure; **fall:** return to Dayton, build a wind tunnel and test 200 different styles of wings.

1902 Return to Kitty Hawk with new glider; this one flies successfully; they make hundreds of controlled flights.

1903 **March:** apply for patent for a "flying machine"; **Sept.:** ship their first powered aircraft, the *Flyer*, to Kitty Hawk; **Dec. 17:** *Flyer* flies for first time, with Orville at controls for 12-second flight; make three more flights before wind gust flips it, damaging it beyond repair.

1904 Move flight test center to Huffman Prairie, Ohio; begin testing *Flyer II*; Wilbur flies first complete circle in history.

1905 **Fall:** Perfect flying machine, *Flyer III*; it completes 24-mile (39-km) flight, staying in air for 38 minutes; **Oct. 5:** last day brothers fly for almost three years; refuse to show plane publicly for fear someone will steal their ideas.

1906 U.S. Patent Office approves Wright brothers' flying machine patent.

1908 **In early part of year,** U.S. military and group of French investors agree to buy Wright aircraft; each buyer wants demonstration of plane's abilities; **April:** brothers travel to Kitty Hawk with new *Wright Model A Flyer*; must relearn how to fly after break of almost three years; **May 4:** friend Charlie Furnas becomes first airplane passenger in history when Wilbur takes him for ride; **summer:** Wilbur stuns French fans with flying talents; becomes international celebrity; **Sept.:** Orville demonstrates *Model A Flyer* to U.S. Army at Fort Myer, Virginia; **Sept. 17:** *Model A* crashes, seriously injuring Orville and killing passenger Lieutenant Thomas Selfridge.

1909 Jan.: Orville and sister Katharine join Wilbur in France; **May:** three return to United States to hero's welcome; **June 10:** President William Taft presents brothers with number of medals, including Congressional Medal of Honor; **June 17–18:** Dayton holds two-day celebration in honor of Wrights; **late June:** Orville pilots plane for first time since accident; **July:** U.S. Army buys *Wright Model A* for $30,000; **Aug.:** brothers launch patent infringement lawsuit against competitor Glenn Curtiss; **Sept.–Oct.:** Wilbur flies circle around Statue of Liberty; flies up and down Hudson River, dazzling millions; **Nov.:** brothers and group of investors open Wright Company.

1910 Open flying school and flight test center; create Wright Fliers aerial exhibition team; judge finds in favor of Wrights in lawsuit against Glenn Curtiss, who files appeal and continues with his aircraft business; brothers unveil two new planes, *Wright Model B,* which will become their most popular aircraft, and *Wright Model R*, a racing plane.

1911 Orville returns to Kitty Hawk to test new glider; Wright Fliers team disbanded after deaths of two pilots.

May 30, 1912 Wilbur Wright dies of typhoid fever; Orville becomes president of the Wright Company.

1913, 1914 Courts side with Wrights in lawsuits against Glenn twice more; Glenn appeals both decisions.

1914 Orville outraged when Smithsonian Institution displays a different aircraft, the *Great Aerodrome,* as world's first craft capable of sustained, controlled, powered flight; Orville, sister Katharine, and father Milton move into Hawthorn Hill, a mansion that Orville designed.

1915 Orville sells Wright Company.

1916 Orville builds Wright Laboratory, a workshop in downtown Dayton; there, he rebuilds original 1903 *Flyer*.

1917 U.S. government forms a patent pool, ending flying machine lawsuits.

1918 Orville pilots a plane for last time.

1928 Out of frustration with the Smithsonian's refusal to recognize *Wright Flyer* as first airplane, Orville ships original *Flyer* to London, where it goes on display at Science Museum.

March 3, 1929 Katharine Wright dies of pneumonia.

1942 Smithsonian finally admits *Flyer* had been world's first flying machine; with World War II on, will be several years before *Flyer* returns to Smithsonian.

January 30, 1948 Orville Wright dies after heart attack.

December 1948 Nearly one year after Orville's death, *Wright Flyer* takes its place at Smithsonian as world's first airplane capable of sustained, controlled, powered flight.

Glossary

adaptation A redesign or reworking of something to meet certain needs

aerodynamics The study of moving air, and the interaction between air and solid bodies moving through it

aeronautical Relating to the science or study of flight

angle of descent The angle at which a plane approaches the runway to land

apprentice A person who learns a trade from a professional in that trade

avian Of or relating to birds

aviator A person who flies or operates an aircraft

biplane An aircraft with two sets of wings, one above the other

conservative Favoring traditional values and ideas and being cautious about change

courier A messenger who transports goods or documents

detractor A person who criticizes or disagrees with someone or something

disposition A person's nature

dissimilar Different

drone A remote-controlled pilotless aircraft

dynamic Relating to an object in motion

elevator A moveable, horizontal surface, usually at the rear of a plane, used to control the plane's pitch, or up-and-down motion along its wing-to-wing axis

embroiled To be deeply involved in a conflict, argument, or other negative situation

endurance The ability to withstand something challenging for a long period of time

equilibrium The balancing of opposing forces, so an object is stable in space

flagrant Obvious, unquestionable; undisguised; shameless (in the case of something considered wrong or immoral)

genealogy A study of a family's ancestors and lineage

gleaning Gathering something from a variety of sources; also, gathering something slowly and methodically

glider An aircraft that flies without an engine

hamper To obstruct or get in the way of

impulsive Acting without forethought

infringe To violate a law or rule

innovation Making changes in something, usually by introducing new methods or ideas

introverted Often shy, more concerned with one's own thoughts than external things

investor Someone who puts his or her own money into a business venture with the expectation of making a profit

lathe A machine used to shape wood by rotating the piece of wood against cutting tools

liberal Open to new ideas or practices that might go against traditional thoughts and behaviors

lift The force that opposes the weight of an aircraft, keeping it in the air

make amends To make up for a wrong done to others

mite A small amount

newfangled Different from what one is used to

perverted Twisted, warped, or distorted from its original shape, meaning, or intent

physics The physical properties of something; the branch of science concerned with matter and energy

pitch The up-and-down motion of the nose of the plane, along its wing-to-wing axis

predicament A difficult, confusing, sometimes embarrassing situation

principle A basic idea or natural law that is important to how a machine is constructed or operated

prone Lying flat, face down

refurbish To redevelop, rebuild, or upgrade

retiring Shy, quiet (as in disposition, or personality)

ridicule To mock or subject someone to scorn

roll The tilt of a plane along its nose-to-tail axis

rudder A moveable, vertical blade at the rear of an aircraft; used for steering and to control the side-to-side slipping, or yaw, of the plane

scornful Mocking or disrespectful

telegram A message sent by telegraphic wire and delivered in printed form

three-axis flight control A method of controlling an aircraft in three dimensions, by managing pitch, roll, and yaw separately

torsion A twisting movement

upbeat Cheerful, positive, optimistic

venue A place where somethng happens, such as an exhibit

whirligig A toy that spins around

wingspan The distance from wingtip to wingtip on an aircraft

yaw Side-to-side slipping of an aircraft, around its vertical axis

Further Information

Books

Crouch, Tom D., and Peter L. Jakab. *The Wright Brothers and the Invention of the Aerial Age*. Washington, D.C.: National Geographic, 2003.

Goldstone, Lawrence. *Birdmen: The Wright Brothers, Glenn Curtiss, and the Battle to Control the Skies*. New York: Ballantine Books, 2014.

Grant, R.G. *Flight: 100 Years of Aviation*. New York: DK Publishing, 2007.

Helfand, Lewis. *The Wright Brothers: A Graphic Novel.* New Delhi, India: Kalyani Navyug Media, 2011.

Videos

Wright Brothers Test Flight, 1909 (online video). History/history.com. This two-minute video from the History cable channel features rare film footage of a Wright brothers 1909 test flight. Watch it for free online at the following link: **www.history.com/topics/inventions/wright-brothers/videos/wright-brothers-test-flight-1909**

The Centennial of Flight: The Wright Math (online video). NASA, 2002. An entertaining and thought-provoking half-hour show about the Wright brothers and how they solved "the flying problem." This NASA Connect video also includes activities related to the Wrights' work. Here is an online link to watch it for free: **http://media.knowitall.org/content/centennial-flight-problem-solving-wright-math**

The Home of the Wright Brothers (online video). Smithsonian, 2013. Produced for the Smithsonian Channel, this video takes a modern look at the Wright brothers' flights and their hometown of Dayton. Watch it at the following link: **www.smithsonianchannel.com/videos/the-home-of-the-wright-brothers/20903**

Ask History: Who Really Invented the Airplane? (online video). History/history. com, 2009. This short video addresses "complicated" questions about the Wright brothers' claim to have invented the first airplane. Watch it here:
www.history.com/topics/inventions/wright-brothers

History of Flight: Part 1 (online video). Warner Pathe News. A six-and-a-half-minute, vintage 1950s-era "News Magazine of the Screen" episode. The film provides classic footage and commentary on the history of flight during, and in the years following, the Wright brothers' earliest experiments with flight. The first four minutes focus on the Wrights. From there, viewers are given glimpses into the development of military aircraft during and after World War I, the use of planes to carry mail, and the role of aircraft in the exploration of Antarctica and other remote locales in the 1920s. You can view the film online at the following link:
www.watchknowlearn.org/Video.aspx?VideoID=3424

Websites

www.wright-brothers.org/
This excellent site, *The Wright Brothers Aeroplane Company: A Virtual Museum of Pioneer Aviation*, offers menu links to a wealth of videos, stories, activities, interviews, photos, and other resources about the Wrights and early aviation.

https://airandspace.si.edu/exhibitions/wright-brothers/online/
The Smithsonian National Air and Space Museum has created this virtual exhibition titled *The Wright Brothers: The Invention of the Aerial Age*. It includes photos and descriptions of the museum's Wright-related artifacts, games, activities, and lots of information about the brothers.

www.nps.gov/wrbr/index.htm
This is the homepage of the Wright Brothers National Memorial at Kill Devil Hills. It includes everything you need to plan your visit or make a virtual visit to the park. It also has a Facebook page:
www.facebook.com/WrightBrothersNMem/?fref=ts

www.aviationtrailinc.org/
The Aviation Trail will take you to all the Wright brothers-related sites in Dayton, Ohio, where the brothers lived most of their lives.

Index

About the Author

Diane Dakers was born and raised in Toronto and now makes her home
in Victoria, British Columbia. She has written two fiction and 15 nonfiction
books for young people. Diane loves finding and telling stories about what
makes people tick—be they world-changers like the Wright brothers,
or lesser-known folks like you and me.